CHOCOLATE

HEAVENLY RECIPES FOR DESSERTS, CAKES AND OTHER DIVINE TREATS

JENNIFER DONOVAN

DUNCAN BAIRD PUBLISHERS

LONDON

Chocolate
Jennifer Donovan

First published in the United Kingdom
and Ireland in 2013
by Duncan Baird Publishers,
an imprint of Watkins Publishing Limited
Sixth Floor
75 Wells Street
London W1T 3QH

A member of Osprey Group

Recipes taken from *The Big Book of Chocolate*,
first published in 2008 by DBP.

Commissioning Editor: Grace Cheetham
Managing Editor: Sarah Epton
Editors: Alison Bolus, Judith More
Managing Designer: Manisha Patel
Design: Gail Jones
Photography: William Lingwood
Food Stylists: Bridget Sargeson, Jayne Cross
Prop Stylists: Helen Trent, Lucy Harvey

For my family: Kevin, Chris and James

A CIP record for this book is available from the
British Library

ISBN: 978-1-84899-102-6

10 9 8 7 6 5 4 3 2 1

Typeset in Goudy Old Style
Colour reproduction by PDQ, UK
Printed in China

Publisher's note: While every care has been
taken in compiling the recipes for this book,
Watkins Publishing Limited, or any other
persons who have been involved in working on
this publication, cannot accept responsibility
for any errors or omissions, inadvertent or
not, that may be found in the recipes or text,
nor for any problems that may arise as a result
of preparing one of these recipes. If you are
pregnant or breastfeeding or have any special
dietary requirements or medical conditions, it
is advisable to consult a medical professional
before following any of the recipes contained
in this book.

UNLESS OTHERWISE STATED:
- Use large eggs
- Do not mix metric and imperial measurements
- 1 tsp = 5ml • 1 tbsp = 15ml • 1 cup = 250ml
- All recipes serve 4

Contents

Introduction

There are few things in the world that evoke such intense emotions as chocolate. Silky, smooth and sensuous, chocolate has been around for centuries. It is thought to have been discovered in Mexico by the Aztec Indians, and then brought to Spain in the 16th century. It is believed that the Aztec Indians first used beans from the cacao tree to make a drink for royal occasions, and that the Spaniards made this bitter drink more palatable by adding cane sugar and spices such as cinnamon and vanilla. By the 17th century, drinking chocolate was fashionable throughout Europe, and by the 19th century chocolate to eat had been developed, and traditional hand-manufacturing methods for making chocolates gave way to mass production.

Today, chocolate has become more popular than ever. Gourmet chocolate boutiques cater for the growing passion for top-quality chocolate. Around the world, consumers are demanding better-sourced and higher-quality ingredients, so Fairtrade chocolate (where the cocoa beans have been sourced direct from farmers at prices that allow the farming communities to thrive and expand) and organic chocolate are both reaching a wider market.

This comprehensive book explains all you need to know about chocolate. It guides the home cook through a range of delicious chocolate recipes, from fabulous home-made cakes, brownies, ice creams, puddings and muffins to spectacular desserts and hand-made chocolates. Some of them will be familiar favourites, while others will provide some new and exciting ways to use chocolate.

As well as providing a wealth of simple-to-follow recipes, and briefly outlining the origins of chocolate, this book explains in simple terms the most common ingredients and methods used when cooking with chocolate – all designed to make the recipes even easier for you to reproduce at home.

WHAT IS CHOCOLATE?

Cocoa beans, from which chocolate is derived, are a product of the cacao tree. This is believed to have originated in the tropical areas of South America, although the exact location is a source of some dispute. A relatively delicate plant, the cacao tree needs protection from wind and a good amount of shade; it usually bears fruit in the fifth year of cultivation in natural conditions. Although there are around 20 different varieties of cacao plant, only three are widely used in the making of chocolate – Forastero, Crillo and Trinitero.

The fruit of the cacao plant, known as 'pods', contain between 20 and 50 cream-coloured beans, and it takes around 400 beans to make just 500g/1lb chocolate. The beans are fermented, dried, cleaned and roasted. Then the roasted beans are ground to produce a thick cacao liquor, or cacao mass, and finally pressed to extract the fat, known as cocoa butter.

Cacao liquor and cocoa butter are the essential ingredients of any chocolate product, and the amount included varies from around 25 per cent of the product's weight up to approximately 80 per cent, occasionally more. Other ingredients, including sugar, vanilla and milk, are added to the chocolate before it goes through the final processing stages. Generally, the sweeter the chocolate, the more sugar has been added and the less cacao liquor and cocoa butter it contains. The darker and more bitter the chocolate, the higher the cacao liquor and cocoa butter content; this is widely considered to be a superior chocolate. However, chocolate preferences vary between individuals, so it is best to experiment with what you have available to see which you prefer.

TYPES OF CHOCOLATE

There are a number of basic categories of chocolate. The first is dark chocolate, sometimes referred to as plain chocolate or couverture. This is designed for both eating and cooking. Look for chocolate with a high cocoa content (usually marked as a percentage on the label). Ideally, the percentage should be somewhere between 70 and 85 per cent, although it is important to remember what you are ultimately using it for. The most readily available chocolate tends to range between 60 and 70 per cent, which renders good results, though higher percentages do exist.

The recipes in this book have all been made from dark chocolate (where specified) with a cocoa butter content of 70 per cent. However, if you want to enjoy the best-quality chocolate straight from the packet, be aware that many people prefer the highest cocoa butter content they can find, which can be up to about 85 per cent. I prefer not to use a chocolate of that percentage for cooking as the result can often be too bitter for a chocolate sauce or cake, which requires a slightly sweeter finish.

Also commonly available is milk chocolate, which generally contains less than 3 per cent cocoa butter, and has sugar, milk powder and vanilla added. Milk chocolate is not as successful in baking and cooking as dark chocolate, but you can happily use it as a substitute in mousses, fillings, drinks and cookies, particularly if they are destined for children, who prefer the less bitter flavour. However, once again, for the tastiest results look for good-quality milk chocolate, as many manufacturers use vegetable oils, artificial flavours, fillers and milk solids in their products. Organic varieties of chocolate make a good choice here.

White chocolate is another widely available product, although it is technically not chocolate at all. This is because white chocolate does not contain cacao liquor, instead being made from cocoa butter, sugar, milk and vanilla. Although not a pure chocolate, white chocolate is still very popular and gives good results in cooking.

Cocoa powder and drinking chocolate are also derived from chocolate. 'Dutch-processed' cocoa, where the cocoa is treated with an alkali to give a slightly different flavour and a darker appearance, is considered to give the best taste. Cocoa powder is derived from the pressed cake that remains after most of the cocoa butter has been removed. It may have 10 per cent or more cocoa butter content. Most commercial drinking chocolate (which is designed to be made into a hot or cold drink) is usually made from a mixture of cocoa powder and sugar. Both cocoa powder and drinking chocolate have their uses in cooking, but, as with chocolate, the quality does vary, so experiment with the different brands and buy the best you can afford.

STORING CHOCOLATE

As a rough guide, chocolate will keep for a year if stored in the correct conditions. Store in a cool place – around 20°C (70°F) – and don't refrigerate it unless the temperature is very hot, as the moist environment of the refrigerator will shorten the life of the chocolate. Chocolate also absorbs the odours of foods stored around it, so be sure to keep it wrapped tightly in plastic film or in a container with a tight-fitting lid.

The white film sometimes found on chocolate that has been stored incorrectly is called a 'bloom'. This is caused by condensation that has melted the surface sugar on the chocolate, and although it will not taste or look as nice as chocolate in good condition, it can still be used for melting or baking.

COOK'S INGREDIENTS

Most of the ingredients used for the recipes in this book are widely available and are often very standard, but it is worth noting a few specific points.

Butter – all recipes, unless otherwise stated, use salted butter.

Eggs – large eggs are used in all the recipes. Some recipes contain raw eggs, which carry a slight risk of salmonella, and should therefore be served with care and not be given to small children, pregnant women or the elderly.

Flour – plain flour and self-raising flour are used throughout this book. Plain flour is also known as all-purpose flour. If you do not have any self-raising, and need to make some, simply add 1½ tsp baking powder and ½ tsp salt to every 125g/4¼oz/1 cup plain flour.

Gold leaf – this is an edible product and is most commonly available from specialist cake-decorating suppliers.

Leaf gelatine – this comes in solid sheets that you soak in cold water until they soften. They dissolve easily in very warm liquid. Where necessary, you can substitute powdered gelatine – 10g/¼oz will set around 500ml/17fl oz/2 cups liquid.

Sugar – caster sugar is used predominantly in the baking section of this book because its fine-grained quality gives the best results.

COOK'S TOOLS

You will not need much specialist equipment when working with chocolate. The recipes in this book use a standard range of kitchen utensils, including loose-bottomed spring-form cake tins and fluted tart tins in a variety of shapes and sizes. However, some items you may not already have do make the process that much easier.

Baking beans – these are ceramic beads that are used to weight a pastry case when baked 'blind', that is, without a filling.

Baking paper (sometimes called baking parchment) – this is used for lining tins and baking trays. It is better than greaseproof paper.

Double boiler – this consists of a saucepan fitted with a smaller pan on top. The base pan holds water, which is heated, while the ingredients sit in the top, away from direct contact with the heat. It is useful for heating and melting delicate ingredients such as chocolate and egg custards.

Electric hand mixer – this will enable you to beat and whisk ingredients with the minimum of effort. Alternatively, use a hand whisk or free-standing electric mixer (where applicable).

Food processor – use this to crush biscuits for crumb crusts and to bind cookie dough, among other culinary jobs.

Baking trays and tins – use nonstick bakeware where possible, ideally silicone, which is durable and flexible. Note that cake and flan tins come in various depths, and it is important to use the recommended depth to avoid having too much or too little filling. Choose tins with loose bottoms for ease.

COOKING TECHNIQUES

Using a bain marie – this French cookery term refers to a 'water bath'. You use this method to cook food in the oven very gently (often fragile dishes such as baked custards) and to prevent overcooking. You place the dish in which the food is cooked inside a larger vessel (sometimes with a cloth underneath to protect the base), which you then fill with water to come half way up the dish.

Melting chocolate – chocolate is a delicate product, and can burn easily. It melts best at temperatures between 40°C/104°F and 45°C/113°F. A double boiler is effective (see above), and prevents the chocolate from overheating, but you can also melt chocolate in a single saucepan directly on the stove over a very low heat, as long as you watch it closely and stir it gently. Alternatively, you can use a microwave oven. As the time needed will vary according to the amount of chocolate to be melted and the power of the oven, it's best to experiment to find out what works best for you. As a guide, use 30-second bursts until the chocolate has melted, stirring gently in between.

Tempering – this is a process involving the heating and cooling of chocolate at specific temperatures, which stabilizes the chocolate and gives it a shiny appearance. It also gives the chocolate a hard texture. Tempering is mainly used by professional chocolate makers, and can be done by hand or by machine. This process is not necessary for the recipes throughout this book.

FINISHING TOUCHES

Chocolate curls, leaves and piped shapes are simple to make and add a special touch to the final product.

Making chocolate curls – a simple way is to sweep a wide-bladed vegetable peeler over a block of chocolate. Keep the chocolate cool, or the curls will lose their shape. A slightly more complicated way is to spread melted chocolate over a marble slab, if you have one, or the back of a large metal baking tray. Leave to cool, and then slide a long-bladed knife along the surface of the chocolate to create a curl. This can take a little practice, but is very rewarding. You can use this technique with dark, milk or white chocolate, or a combination of two or more, which can look quite impressive.

Making chocolate leaves – simply brush melted chocolate on the back of a clean, well-defined leaf and chill. When cold, simply peel off the leaf, leaving a delicate imprint of veins on the chocolate.

Piping chocolate shapes and lines – you can pipe chocolate shapes with a fine nozzle on to baking paper – but don't make them too delicate, or they will fall apart. Chill, then lift off as required. You can also randomly pipe lines of dark and white chocolate quite densely over baking paper, then set aside to chill, and break off pieces as required. This is a simple and effective method of decorating ice creams, mousses and meringues.

Chocolate crumb crust

PREPARATION TIME 10 minutes   COOKING TIME 10 minutes   MAKES 1 x 23cm/9in crumb crust

250g/9oz digestive biscuits
2 tbsp cocoa powder
100g/3½oz butter, melted

1 Preheat the oven to 200°C/400°F/gas 6.

2 Break up the biscuits roughly with your hands and then pulse them in a food processor (or place them in a plastic bag and crush with a rolling pin) until they are fine crumbs. Add the cocoa and melted butter, and pulse until the mixture is well combined.

3 Empty the mixture into a greased 23cm/9in spring-form cake tin, press it over the base and up the sides of the tin (according to the recipe), and bake in the hot oven for 10 minutes. Remove from the oven and leave the crust to cool completely before removing it from the tin.

Creamy thick chocolate custard

PREPARATION TIME 10 minutes   COOKING TIME 10 minutes   MAKES 750ml/26fl oz/3 cups

375ml/13fl oz/1½ cups milk
375ml/13fl oz/1½ cups double
  cream
8 egg yolks
150g/5½oz/⅔ cup caster sugar
2 tbsp cocoa powder
1 tsp vanilla essence

1 In a small saucepan, heat the milk and cream over a low heat, until just warm. In a large bowl, whisk the egg yolks, sugar and cocoa together, using a hand whisk, then whisk in the warm milk mixture. Return the mixture to the pan with the vanilla essence, and stir constantly with a wooden spoon until the mixture begins to thicken and coats the back of the spoon. Do not boil.

2 Transfer to a clean bowl and leave to cool completely.

Fresh caramel sauce

PREPARATION TIME 5 minutes   COOKING TIME 5 minutes   MAKES 500ml/17fl oz/2 cups

125g/4½oz/½ cup plus 2 tsp
   caster sugar
125g/4½oz butter, chopped
250ml/9fl oz/1 cup double
   cream

1   In a medium-sized saucepan, stir together the sugar and butter over a low heat until they melt, using a wooden spoon. Continue stirring gently until the mixture becomes a light caramel colour.

2   Remove the pan from the heat and add the cream (taking care not to burn your hand, as the sugar mixture will spatter), then return the pan to the heat and stir until well combined.

3   Pour the sauce into an airtight jar and set aside to cool completely before placing in the refrigerator. It will keep for 2–3 days.

Choux pastry

PREPARATION TIME 10 minutes   COOKING TIME 5 minutes   MAKES 6 large éclairs or 12 profiteroles

2 tsp caster sugar
60g/2¼oz chilled butter,
   chopped
90g/3¼oz/¾ cup plain flour,
   sifted
2 eggs, lightly beaten

1   In a medium-sized saucepan, combine the sugar, butter and 185ml/6fl oz/¾ cup water over a low heat, and stir until the butter has just melted. Remove from the heat and add all the flour to the butter mixture, stirring well with a wooden spoon (the mixture will form a thick dough.)

2   Return the saucepan to the heat and continue stirring for 1 minute, or until the dough comes away from the sides of the saucepan.

3   Remove the saucepan from the heat and beat in the eggs, using an electric hand mixer. For best results, use the dough while still warm.

Sweet shortcrust pastry

PREPARATION TIME 10 minutes, plus chilling   COOKING TIME 30–35 minutes

MAKES 1 x 23cm/9in pastry case or 4–6 individual pastry cases

250g/9oz/2 cups plain flour,
   plus extra for rolling out
3 tbsp icing sugar
150g/5½oz chilled butter,
   chopped
2 egg yolks

1   In a large bowl, combine the flour and icing sugar. Add the butter and rub it in with your fingertips until it forms small crumbs. (Alternatively, do this in a food processor, but work quickly or the pastry will be tough.) Work in the egg yolks and just enough of 2 tbsp iced water to form a dough, using a flat-bladed knife or spatula. Note that the less water you use, the more tender the pastry will be. Wrap the dough in plastic film and refrigerate for 15 minutes.

2   Preheat the oven to 180°C/350°F/gas 4. Roll out the pastry on a lightly floured surface to roughly 5mm/¼in thick, to fit a 23cm/9in fluted loose-bottomed tart tin, 3–4cm/1½in deep. Place the pastry in the tin to form a pastry case, taking care not to stretch it, and trim around the edge.

3   Line the pastry case with baking paper and fill with baking beans. Cook in the hot oven for 20-25 minutes, then remove from the oven and gently lift out the paper and beans. Return the tin to the oven for a further 8-10 minutes, or until the pastry is dry and golden brown. (Alternatively, divide the pastry into 4 or 6 pieces and roll each one out to fit a 10cm/4in fluted loose-bottomed tart tin, 3-4cm/1½in deep, and cook for 10-12 minutes, then a further 5-7 minutes.)

variation *To make Chocolate Shortcrust Pastry, add 1 tbsp cocoa powder with the flour and cook the pastry until it is dry and dark brown.*

Quick-fix desserts

This chapter
offers a selection of
superb desserts that can be
made in a flash with the minimum
of fuss and effort. From White
Chocolate & Raspberry Eton Mess to
Chocolate Zabaglione, these simple
and easy recipes are a delight to
make and are just as impressive
as any time-consuming
creation.

Chocolate zabaglione

PREPARATION TIME 10 minutes   COOKING TIME 7–8 minutes

8 egg yolks
4 tbsp caster sugar
5 tbsp Marsala wine
100g/3½oz dark chocolate,
    melted and left to cool
4 sponge-finger biscuits

1   In a large, heatproof bowl, beat together the yolks, sugar and Marsala wine, using an electric hand mixer. Place the bowl over a pan of gently simmering water (making sure that the bowl does not touch the water or the eggs will scramble). Whisk vigorously until the mixture is frothy and just starting to thicken (this will take around 7–8 minutes), using a hand whisk.

2   Remove the bowl from the heat and beat in the melted chocolate, using an electric hand mixer.

3   Using a large spoon, divide the mixture evenly between 4 dishes. Serve immediately, accompanied by the sponge-finger biscuits.

Chocolate & chestnut mess

PREPARATION TIME 10 minutes

300ml/10½fl oz/1¼ cups
    double cream
6 tbsp tinned, sweetened
    chestnut purée
125g/4½oz dark chocolate,
    grated
2 tbsp coffee liqueur
1 tbsp caster sugar
8 crispy-style meringues

1   In a large bowl, whip the cream and chestnut purée until the mixture is just beginning to thicken, using an electric hand mixer. Add 100g/3½oz of the grated chocolate, the liqueur and sugar and whip until the mixture is smooth and holds its shape lightly (taking care not to over-whip).

2   Put the meringues in a plastic bag, crush them lightly with a rolling pin, then empty them into the cream mixture and fold in, using a metal spoon.

3   Spoon the mixture into 4 dishes and sprinkle the remaining grated chocolate over the top.

White chocolate & raspberry Eton mess

PREPARATION TIME 10 minutes

300ml/10fl oz/1¼ cups
  double cream
1 tbsp caster sugar
2 tbsp raspberry liqueur
8 crispy-style meringues
100g/3½oz white chocolate,
  melted and left to cool
125g/4½oz/1 cup raspberries,
  lightly crushed

1   In a large bowl, whip the cream, sugar and liqueur together until the mixture just forms soft peaks, using an electric hand mixer.

2   Put the meringues in a plastic bag, crush them lightly with a rolling pin, then empty them into the cream mixture and mix together, using a wooden spoon. Fold in the melted chocolate and raspberries.

3   Spoon the mixture into 4 dishes and serve immediately.

Chocolate liqueur fondue

PREPARATION TIME 10 minutes   COOKING TIME 5 minutes

300g/10½oz dark chocolate,
    broken into pieces
200ml/7fl oz/¾ cup double
    cream
1 tsp instant coffee granules
1 tbsp coffee or hazelnut
    liqueur
1 tsp vanilla essence
sponge-finger biscuits, for
    dipping

1 In a medium-sized saucepan, heat the chocolate,
cream and coffee together over a low heat until the
chocolate has just melted. Remove the pan from the heat
and stir the mixture with a wooden spoon until smooth.
Stir in the liqueur and the vanilla essence.

2 Pour the fondue into a fondue bowl or small dish
and serve immediately with the sponge-finger biscuits
for dipping.

Quick tiramisu with chocolate

PREPARATION TIME 10 minutes

200g/7oz mascarpone cheese,
softened
2 egg yolks
100g/3½oz/¾ cup plus 1 tbsp
icing sugar, sifted
200ml/7fl oz/1 cup double
cream
100g/3½oz dark or plain
chocolate, melted and left
to cool
6 sponge-finger biscuits
125ml/4fl oz/½ cup strong
coffee
4 tbsp Marsala wine
4 tbsp chocolate shavings

1   In a large bowl, beat the mascarpone, egg yolks and icing sugar together, using an electric hand mixer. Blend in the cream and melted chocolate.

2   Break the sponge-finger biscuits up into small pieces and divide them evenly between 4 dishes.

3   In a small jug, combine the coffee and Marsala wine and pour over the sponge mixture, then spoon over the mascarpone mixture. Top with the chocolate shavings before serving.

Quickest-ever dark chocolate mousse

PREPARATION TIME 10 minutes, plus chilling

2 egg whites
5 tbsp caster sugar
200g/7oz dark chocolate,
    melted and left to cool
250ml/9fl oz/1 cup double
    cream, whipped to soft
    peaks

1 In a large bowl, whisk the egg whites until soft peaks form, using an electric hand mixer. Add the sugar gradually while continuing to whisk until the whites are thick and shiny. Using a metal spoon, fold in the melted chocolate and cream.

2 Using a large spoon, divide the mousse between 4 dishes, and refrigerate for 30 minutes before serving.

Strawberries Romanoff with white chocolate

PREPARATION TIME 40 minutes, plus chilling

300g/10½oz/2 cups
  strawberries, hulled
  and sliced
2 tbsp orange liqueur
2 tbsp icing sugar
250ml/9fl oz/1 cup double
  cream
1 tbsp caster sugar
100g/3½oz white chocolate,
  melted and cooled

1 In a large bowl, stir together the strawberries, liqueur and icing sugar. Refrigerate the mixture for 30 minutes to allow the flavours to mingle.

2 In a clean bowl, whisk the double cream and caster sugar together to form soft peaks, using an electric hand mixer, then stir in the melted chocolate. Purée half of the strawberry mixture in a blender, then, using a metal spoon, gently fold it into the cream mixture with the remaining strawberries.

3 Divide the mixture evenly between 4 dishes.

Roast figs with chocolate sauce

PREPARATION TIME 10 minutes   COOKING TIME 15–20 minutes

75g/2¾oz butter, plus extra
   for greasing
8 large figs
2 tbsp caster sugar
250ml/9fl oz/1 cup double
   cream, whipped to soft
   peaks
1 recipe quantity Rich
   Chocolate Sauce (see
   page 188)

1   Preheat the oven to 180°C/350°F/gas 4. Grease an ovenproof dish (large enough to hold the figs) with butter.
2   Cut a cross in the top of each fig, taking care to keep the fig in one piece. Divide the butter into 8 pieces, and place one piece inside each fig. Place the figs in the prepared dish and sprinkle over the caster sugar.
3   Bake in the hot oven for 15–20 minutes, or until the figs are soft but still hold their shape. Remove from the oven and set the baked figs aside in the dish to cool for 10 minutes.
4   Divide the figs between 4 plates, top with a spoonful of cream, and pour over the rich chocolate sauce.

150

Chocolate heaven desserts

While chocolate cakes, bakes and desserts are, by their very nature, heavenly, sometimes the occasion calls for something just a little extra-special. The recipes in this chapter take chocolate that one step further – they are perfect for a special celebration or for when you just feel like being a bit more indulgent...

Mocha marble cheesecake

PREPARATION TIME 25 minutes, plus chilling   COOKING TIME 40–45 minutes

MAKES 1 x 23cm/9in cheesecake

butter, for greasing
1 recipe quantity Chocolate
  Crumb Crust (see page 13)
300g/10½oz cream cheese,
  softened
200g/7oz ricotta cheese
200g/7oz/¾ cup plus 2 tbsp
  caster sugar
3 tsp cornflour
3 eggs, lightly beaten
2 tsp vanilla essence
500ml/17fl oz/2 cups crème
  fraîche
250ml/9fl oz/1 cup double
  cream
2 tsp instant coffee granules
2 tbsp coffee liqueur
100g/3½oz dark chocolate,
  melted and left to cool

1   Preheat the oven to 170°C/325°F/gas 3. Grease a 23cm/9in spring-form cake tin with butter, and press the prepared chocolate crumb crust into the base.

2   In a large bowl, beat the cream cheese, ricotta and sugar together, using an electric hand mixer, until smooth. Add the cornflour, eggs and vanilla essence, and beat until just combined, then stir in the crème fraîche and cream. Divide the mixture evenly between 2 jugs. Blend the coffee, liqueur and melted chocolate into one half of the mixture, using the electric hand mixer, and leave the other half plain.

3   Pour both of the mixtures over the crumb crust base (use two hands and do this at the same time, if possible). Using a fork, swirl the mixtures together to create a marbled effect.

4   Bake in the hot oven for 40–45 minutes, or until the cheesecake is firm around the edges but still slightly wobbly in the middle. Remove from the oven and leave in the tin to cool completely.

5   Refrigerate the cheesecake for 2 hours or overnight, then remove from the tin.

Mini white chocolate cheesecakes

PREPARATION TIME 30 minutes, plus chilling   COOKING TIME 20–25 minutes

MAKES 6 mini cheesecakes

butter, for greasing
½ recipe quantity Chocolate
   Crumb Crust (see page 13)
200g/7oz cream cheese,
   softened
5 tbsp caster sugar
1 egg, lightly beaten
125g/4½oz white chocolate,
   melted and left to cool
100ml/3½fl oz/⅓ cup double
   cream

1   Preheat the oven to 180°C/350°F/gas 4. Grease 6 holes of a large muffin tin with butter, and line each with a strip of baking paper, extending it up the sides. Divide the crumb crust mixture evenly between the holes and press down firmly to form the cheesecake bases.
2   In a large bowl, beat the cream cheese and sugar together until light and fluffy, using an electric hand mixer, then beat in the egg. Stir in the melted chocolate and cream, using a wooden spoon, then divide the mixture between the holes.
3   Bake in the hot oven for 20–25 minutes, or until the cheesecakes are just set and beginning to brown. Remove from the oven and leave in the tin to cool for 15 minutes.
4   Remove the cheesecakes from the tin, using the strips of baking paper to help you, transfer to individual plates and leave to cool completely. Chill for 1 hour before serving.

Raspberry ripple white chocolate cheesecake

PREPARATION TIME 25 minutes, plus chilling   COOKING TIME 45–50 minutes

MAKES 1 x 23cm/9in cheesecake

butter, for greasing
1 recipe quantity Chocolate
  Crumb Crust (see page 13)
500g/1lb 2oz cream cheese,
  softened
200g/7oz/¾ cup plus 2 tbsp
  caster sugar
2 tbsp plain flour
4 eggs, lightly beaten
250g/9oz white chocolate,
  melted and left to cool
2 tsp vanilla essence
125ml/4fl oz/½ cup double
  cream
125g/4½oz/1 cup raspberries,
  puréed

1 Preheat the oven to 180°C/350°F/gas 4. Grease a 23cm/9in spring-form cake tin with butter, and press the prepared chocolate crumb crust into the base.

2 In a large bowl, beat the cream cheese and sugar together until light and creamy, using an electric hand mixer. Add the flour, eggs, melted chocolate and vanilla essence, and beat until just combined. Stir in the cream. Gently swirl through the raspberry purée, using a wooden spoon and taking care not to over-mix. Pour the filling mixture over the crumb crust base.

3 Bake in the hot oven for 45–50 minutes, or until the cheesecake is firm around the edges but still slightly wobbly in the middle. Remove from the oven and leave in the tin to cool completely.

4 Refrigerate the cheesecake for 2 hours or overnight, then remove from the tin.

White chocolate & lime tart

PREPARATION TIME 15 minutes, plus chilling   COOKING TIME 5 minutes

MAKES 1 x 23cm/9in cake

200ml/7fl oz¾ cup double
   cream
300g/10½oz white chocolate,
   broken into pieces
zest of 2 limes, plus 1 lime,
   thinly sliced
1 recipe quantity Chocolate
   Crumb Crust, baked (see
   page 13)

1 In a small saucepan, heat the cream and chocolate together over a low heat until the chocolate has just melted, then remove from the heat and stir until smooth, using a wooden spoon. Stir in the lime zest, then set aside to cool for 10 minutes.

2 Pour the mixture into the baked crumb crust, and refrigerate for 2 hours or until set. Decorate with lime slices before serving.

Profiteroles with coffee cream & chocolate sauce

PREPARATION TIME 40 minutes   COOKING TIME 20–25 minutes

MAKES 12 profiteroles

1 recipe quantity Choux Pastry (see page 14)

250ml/9fl oz/1 cup double cream

2 tsp instant coffee granules

1 tbsp coffee liqueur

2 tbsp caster sugar

1 recipe quantity Rich Chocolate Sauce (see page 188)

1 Preheat the oven to 220°C/425°F/gas 7. Line a large baking tray with baking paper. Spoon 12 tablespoonfuls of the choux pastry on the baking tray. Sprinkle lightly with water.

2 Bake in the hot oven for 20–25 minutes, or until the profiteroles are a deep golden brown. It is important to make sure that the middles are as dry as possible to achieve the best result.

3 Remove the profiteroles from the oven and transfer to a wire rack. Pierce each profiterole with a small, sharp knife to make a tiny hole through which the steam can escape. Leave to cool completely, then split widthways and, if any wet dough remains, scrape it out.

4 For the filling, put the cream, coffee, liqueur and sugar in a bowl and whip to soft peaks, using an electric hand mixer. Spoon the creamy filling into the profiteroles. Place 3 profiteroles on each plate and pour over the chocolate sauce.

Strawberry & chocolate mille-feuilles

PREPARATION TIME 45 minutes, plus cooling   COOKING TIME 15–20 minutes

375g/13oz ready-rolled
  puff pastry
2 tbsp milk
4 tsp caster sugar
250ml/9fl oz/1 cup double
  cream, whipped to soft
  peaks
150g/5½oz/1 cup strawberries,
  hulled and thinly sliced
100g/3½oz dark or milk
  chocolate, melted and left
  to cool
icing sugar, sifted, for dusting

1   Preheat the oven to 190°C/375°F/gas 5. Roll the pastry out on a lightly floured surface to 1cm/½in thick. Cut into 8 rectangles, each approximately 10 x 7cm/ 4 x 2¾in. Place the rectangles on a large baking tray, and lightly brush the top of each one with milk. Using a fork, prick the pastry in 5 or 6 places, then sprinkle with caster sugar.

2   Bake the rectangles in the hot oven for 15–20 minutes, or until the pastry has risen and is golden brown. Remove from the oven, and leave the rectangles on the baking tray to cool completely.

3   To assemble the mille-feuilles, place a rectangle on each plate and spread over a spoonful of whipped cream. Top the cream with one-eighth of the strawberries and drizzle over one-eighth of the melted chocolate. Repeat with a second set of layers – pastry, cream, strawberries and chocolate – then dust the mille-feuilles with icing sugar and serve immediately.

Chocolate nut bavarois

PREPARATION TIME 25 minutes, plus cooling and chilling   COOKING TIME 5 minutes

200ml/7fl oz/¾ cup milk
2 tbsp chocolate hazelnut
    paste
2 tbsp hazelnut liqueur
100g/3½oz dark or milk
    chocolate, broken
    into pieces
3 sheets leaf gelatine
4 egg yolks
3 tbsp plus 1 tsp caster sugar
250ml/9fl oz/1 cup double
    cream, whipped to soft
    peaks
chocolate curls, to sprinkle
    (optional)

1   In a medium-sized saucepan, heat the milk, chocolate hazelnut paste, liqueur and chocolate over a low heat until the chocolate has melted, stirring constantly with a wooden spoon. Remove from the heat and stir until smooth, then set aside to cool.

2   Meanwhile, soak the gelatine sheets in a bowl of cold water for 5–10 minutes until soft, then remove them, wring out any excess water and stir into the chocolate mixture until they dissolve. In a clean bowl, beat the egg yolks and sugar together, using a hand whisk, then gradually add to the cooled chocolate mixture. Pour into a clean bowl and set aside for approximately 1½ hours until cool and beginning to thicken.

3   Gently fold in the cream, using a metal spoon, then pour the mixture into a 500ml/17fl oz/2 cup capacity jelly mould. Refrigerate for 3 hours or overnight. Sprinkle with chocolate curls, if wanted, before serving.

White chocolate panna cottas

PREPARATION TIME 15 minutes, plus cooling and chilling   COOKING TIME 5 minutes

3 sheets leaf gelatine
250ml/9fl oz/1 cup double
  cream
125ml/4fl oz/½ cup milk
100g/3½oz white chocolate,
  broken into pieces
2 tbsp caster sugar
1 tsp vanilla essence
125g/4½oz/1 cup raspberries
2 tbsp icing sugar, sifted

1 Soak the gelatine sheets in a bowl of cold water for
5–10 minutes until soft.

2 In a small saucepan, heat the cream, milk, chocolate,
sugar and vanilla essence together over a low heat until
the chocolate has just melted. Remove from the heat
and stir with a wooden spoon until smooth. Remove
the gelatine from the water and wring out any excess.
Drop the gelatine into the cream mixture and stir briefly
until dissolved.

3 Divide the mixture evenly between 4 x 125ml/4fl oz/
½ cup capacity moulds on a tray, and set aside to cool for
approximately 30 minutes. Refrigerate the panna cottas
for 3 hours or overnight.

4 In a blender, pulse the raspberries to a purée with the
icing sugar to make a coulis. Dip the moulds briefly into
hot water and run a sharp knife around the sides. Turn the
panna cottas out on to 4 plates and serve with the coulis.

White chocolate mousse with raspberries

PREPARATION TIME 20 minutes, plus chilling   COOKING TIME 5 minutes

200g/7oz/1½ cups
    raspberries, plus extra
    for serving (optional)
150ml/5fl oz/⅔ cup milk
200g/7oz white chocolate,
    broken into pieces
1 tsp vanilla essence
2 sheets leaf gelatine
200ml/7fl oz/¾ cup double
    cream, whipped to soft
    peaks
chocolate curls, for decorating

1   Divide the raspberries evenly between 4 small glasses. In a small saucepan, heat the milk, white chocolate and vanilla essence over a low heat until the chocolate has just melted, stirring frequently with a wooden spoon.

2   In a small bowl, soak the gelatine in cold water until soft. Remove the gelatine from the bowl and squeeze out any excess water, then stir the gelatine into the chocolate milk until dissolved. Pour into a clean bowl, and set aside until cool and beginning to thicken. Fold the whipped cream into the chocolate mixture using a metal spoon, then spoon the resulting mousse over the raspberries in the glasses. Refrigerate for 3 hours or overnight.

3   Use the chocolate curls and the extra raspberries, if using, to decorate the top of each mousse.

Black cherry trifle

PREPARATION TIME 30 minutes, plus chilling   MAKES 4–6

200g/7oz trifle sponges or
  plain cake, sliced
4 tbsp cherry brandy
400g/14oz/2 cups tinned
  cherries, drained, syrup
  reserved
1 recipe quantity Creamy
  Thick Chocolate Custard
  (see page 13)
250ml/9fl oz/1 cup double
  cream
2 tbsp caster sugar
100g/3½oz dark chocolate,
  melted and left to cool
6 ripe cherries

1   Place the trifle sponges or sliced cake into the base of
a large serving bowl and sprinkle over the cherry brandy.
Scatter the tinned cherries over the sponge base, along
with 4 tbsp of the reserved syrup, then top with the
creamy thick chocolate custard.

2   In a large bowl, whip the cream with the sugar until
thick but not too stiff, using an electric hand mixer, then
spread it over the custard in the bowl. Drizzle over half of
the melted chocolate. Refrigerate the trifle for 2 hours
or overnight.

3   Meanwhile, half-dip the cherries in the remaining
melted chocolate, leave them to set on baking paper and
then use to decorate the trifle.

Dark chocolate tiramisu

PREPARATION TIME 20 minutes, plus chilling   SERVES 4–6

2 eggs, separated, plus
   3 yolks
100g/3½oz/⅓ cup plus 4 tsp
   caster sugar
250g/9oz mascarpone cheese,
   softened
100g/3½oz dark chocolate,
   melted and cooled, plus 4
   tbsp grated
350ml/12fl oz/1½ cups strong
   coffee
4 tbsp Marsala wine
20 sponge-finger biscuits
2 tbsp cocoa powder, sifted

1   In a large bowl, beat all the egg yolks and the sugar together until light and creamy, using an electric hand mixer. Blend in the mascarpone and melted chocolate until combined. In a clean bowl, whisk the egg whites until stiff but not dry, using clean attachments for the electric hand mixer, then, using a metal spoon, fold the whisked whites into the mascarpone mixture.

2   In a clean bowl, combine the coffee and Marsala wine and dip the sponge-finger biscuits into the mixture, allowing them to soak up some of the liquid.

3   Use 10 of the soaked biscuits to line the base of a serving dish approximately 28 x 18 x 6cm/11 x 7 x 2½in. Pour half the mascarpone mixture over the biscuit layer. Cover with the remaining biscuits, then the remaining mascarpone. Dust the top with cocoa and sprinkle over the grated chocolate. Refrigerate for 2 hours before serving.

Passionfruit, white chocolate & strawberry meringue roulade

PREPARATION TIME 25 minutes, plus cooling   COOKING TIME 15–18 minutes   SERVES 4–6

melted butter, for greasing
4 egg whites
pinch salt
250g/9oz/1 cup plus 4 tsp
    caster sugar
250ml/9fl oz/1 cup double
    cream, whipped to soft
    peaks
150g/5½oz white chocolate,
    melted and left to cool
300g/10½oz/2 cups
    strawberries, hulled
    and sliced
4 passionfruit
icing sugar, sifted, for dusting

1   Preheat the oven to 170°C/325°F/gas 3. Line a 33 x 23cm/13 x 9in Swiss roll tin with baking paper, so that the paper hangs over the edge. Lightly grease the paper with melted butter.

2   In a large bowl, whisk the egg whites with the salt until soft peaks form, using an electric hand mixer, then gradually add the sugar and continue whisking until stiff. Spread the meringue mixture over the prepared tin, using a palette knife.

3   Bake in the hot oven for 15–18 minutes, or until the surface is crisp. Remove from the oven and leave to cool completely in the tin.

4   Turn the roulade out on to a large piece of baking paper and peel off the lining paper. In a large bowl, fold the cream and melted chocolate together, using a metal spoon. Using a palette knife, spread the cream mixture evenly over the roulade, then cover with the strawberries. Remove the pulp from the passionfruit, using a sharp knife, and scatter it over the strawberries.

5   Using the paper to help you, but making sure that it does not get trapped inside the roulade, gradually roll up the meringue Swiss-roll style from a short end. Transfer carefully to a serving plate and dust with icing sugar before serving.

Chocolate meringues with blackberries

PREPARATION TIME 15 minutes, plus cooling   COOKING TIME 40 minutes

MAKES 8–10 meringues

3 egg whites
150g/5½oz/⅔ cup caster sugar
50g/1¾oz dark chocolate, grated, plus 50g/1¾oz melted and left to cool
1 tsp cocoa powder
1 recipe quantity Chocolate Chantilly Cream (see page 194)
185g/6½oz/1½ cups blackberries
icing sugar, sifted, for dusting

1   Preheat the oven to 140°C/275°F/gas 1. Line 2 baking trays with baking paper.

2   In a bowl, whisk the egg whites until stiff peaks form, using an electric hand mixer, then gradually whisk in the sugar until the mixture is thick and shiny and the sugar has dissolved. Gently fold in the grated chocolate and cocoa, using a metal spoon. Place 16–20 heaped tablespoonfuls of the meringue mixture on the prepared trays.

3   Bake in the warm oven for 40 minutes, then turn the oven off and leave the meringues in the oven to cool completely.

4   Remove the meringues from the oven, and sandwich them together in pairs with the chocolate Chantilly cream. Divide between 4 plates, and drizzle over the melted chocolate. Serve with the blackberries, dusted with icing sugar.

Irish coffee meringue with chocolate

PREPARATION TIME 30 minutes, plus cooling   COOKING TIME 60 minutes

MAKES 1 x 23cm/9in cake

6 egg whites
300g/10½oz/1⅓ cups caster
    sugar
1 tbsp instant coffee granules
1 tbsp cocoa powder
375ml/13fl oz/1½ cups double
    cream
2 tbsp coffee liqueur
100g/3½oz dark chocolate,
    melted and cooled

1   Preheat the oven to 100°C/200°F/gas ½. Line 2 oven trays with baking paper, and draw 2 x 23cm/9in circles on the paper in pencil.

2   In a bowl, whisk the egg whites until stiff peaks form, using an electric hand mixer, then gradually whisk in the sugar until the mixture is thick and shiny and the sugar has dissolved. Whisk in the coffee and cocoa. Spoon on to the prepared trays and, using a palette knife, spread over the circles on the baking paper.

3   Bake in the warm oven for 60 minutes until the meringue is crisp but not brown. Remove from the oven, and leave the meringues to cool completely on the trays.

4   In a clean bowl, whisk the cream and liqueur together, using an electric hand mixer, to form soft peaks. To assemble the meringue, place 1 round on a serving tray, spread over half the liqueur cream and drizzle over half the melted chocolate. Repeat with the second meringue, remaining cream and chocolate for the top layer, then refrigerate the meringue for 2 hours before serving.

Chilled chocolate & raspberry soufflés

PREPARATION TIME 30 minutes, plus chilling   COOKING TIME 5 minutes

250ml/9fl oz/1 cup milk
75g/2¾oz dark chocolate, broken into pieces
3 egg yolks
4 tbsp caster sugar
3 sheets leaf gelatine
125ml/4fl oz/½ cup puréed raspberries
200ml/7fl oz/¾ cup double cream, whipped to soft peaks

1   Prepare 4 x 150ml/5fl oz/⅔ cup capacity soufflé dishes by wrapping a 5cm/2in wide strip of foil around the outside of each dish, tying it in place with string. The foil should stand 2cm/¾in above the rim of the dish.

2   In a small saucepan, heat the milk and chocolate together over a low heat until just melted, then remove the pan from the heat and stir with a wooden spoon until smooth. In a large bowl, whisk the yolks and sugar together, using an electric hand mixer, then whisk in the warm chocolate milk. Return the pan to the heat and continue cooking, stirring constantly with a wooden spoon, until the mixture thickens and coats the back of the spoon. Do not allow to boil.

3   Meanwhile, in a bowl, soak the gelatine sheets in cold water for 5-10 minutes until soft, then remove them, wring out any excess water and stir into the warm custard until they dissolve. Pour the mixture into a clean bowl and leave to cool.

4   Gently fold the raspberry purée and cream into the cooled custard, using a metal spoon, then divide equally between the prepared dishes. Refrigerate for 2 hours or overnight. Remove the foil collars before serving.

Hot chocolate soufflés

PREPARATION TIME 25 minutes   COOKING TIME 20–23 minutes

melted butter, for greasing
80g/2¾oz/⅓ cup caster sugar,
   plus extra for coating
2 tbsp cornflour
250ml/9fl oz/1 cup milk
100g/3½oz dark chocolate,
   broken into pieces
3 eggs, separated, plus
   2 whites
icing sugar, sifted, for dusting

1 Preheat the oven to 190°C/375°F/gas 5. Grease 4 x 200ml/7fl oz/¾ cup capacity ovenproof cups with melted butter and coat lightly with sugar.

2 In a small bowl, mix the cornflour to a paste with 2 tbsp of the milk. In a medium-sized saucepan, heat the remaining milk with the chocolate and 3 tbsp plus 1 tsp of the sugar over a low heat. When the chocolate has melted, whisk in the cornflour paste, using a hand whisk. Continue whisking until the mixture boils and thickens, then turn down to a simmer and cook for 1 minute more. Remove from the heat and allow to cool for a few minutes before beating in the egg yolks. Set the mixture aside to cool completely.

3 In a large bowl, whisk all the egg whites to soft peaks, using an electric hand mixer, then add the remaining sugar and continue to whisk until stiff but not dry. Gently fold the whisked whites into the chocolate mixture, using a metal spoon, and divide equally between the cups.

4 Bake in the hot oven for 15–18 minutes, or until the soufflés are well risen. Remove from the oven, dust with icing sugar and serve immediately.

Chocolate roulade with mixed berries & white chocolate cream

PREPARATION TIME 25 minutes   COOKING TIME 18–20 minutes   SERVES 4–6

butter, for greasing
175g/6oz/¾ cup caster sugar
6 eggs, separated
175g/6oz dark chocolate,
    melted and left to cool
2 tbsp cocoa powder
250ml/9fl oz/1 cup double
    cream, whipped to soft
    peaks
100g/3½oz white chocolate,
    melted and left to cool
185g/6½oz/1½ cups mixed
    berries
icing sugar, sifted, for dusting

1 Preheat the oven to 180°C/350°F/gas 4. Grease a
33 x 23cm/13 x 9in Swiss roll tin with butter, and line
the base and sides with baking paper.

2 In a large bowl, beat the sugar and egg yolks together,
using an electric hand mixer, until thick and creamy. Stir
in the melted dark chocolate and cocoa, using a wooden
spoon. In a clean bowl, whisk the egg whites until stiff
but not dry, using clean attachments for the electric hand
mixer, then gently fold into the chocolate mixture, using a
metal spoon. Pour the mixture into the prepared tin and
spread evenly, using a palette knife.

3 Bake in the hot oven for 18–20 minutes, or until firm.
Remove from the oven and leave to cool completely in
the tin. When cool, turn out on to a clean tea towel and
remove the lining paper.

4 In a large bowl, fold the cream and the melted white
chocolate together, using a metal spoon, and spread evenly
over the roulade. Scatter over the mixed berries, slicing
any strawberries.

5 Using the tea towel to help you, but making sure that
it does not get trapped inside the roulade, gradually roll
up the roulade Swiss roll style from a short end. Transfer
carefully to a serving plate, and dust with icing sugar
before serving.

Sticky chocolate cake

PREPARATION TIME 25 minutes   COOKING TIME 50–55 minutes

MAKES 1 x 23cm/9in cake

250g/9oz butter, plus extra
    for greasing
250ml/9fl oz/1 cup double
    cream
175g/6oz dark chocolate,
    broken into pieces
1 tsp instant coffee granules
250g/9oz/1 cup soft brown
    sugar
4 eggs, lightly beaten
2 tsp vanilla essence
200g/7oz/1½ cups plus 4 tsp
    self-raising flour
1 tsp cinnamon
1 tsp nutmeg
125g/4½oz/1 cup raisins
115g/4oz/¾ cup plus 2 tbsp
    walnuts, chopped
1 recipe quantity Rich
    Chocolate Sauce (see
    page 188)

1   Preheat the oven to 170°F/325°C/gas 3. Grease a
23cm/9in spring-form cake tin with butter, and line the
base with baking paper.

2   In a small saucepan, heat the cream, chocolate and
coffee over a low heat until the chocolate has just melted.
Remove the pan from the heat, and stir the mixture with
a wooden spoon until smooth, then leave to cool. In a
large bowl, beat the butter and sugar together, using an
electric hand mixer, until light and creamy, then beat
in the eggs gradually. Stir in the vanilla essence and
chocolate mixture, using a wooden spoon. Gently fold in
the flour, cinnamon, nutmeg, raisins and walnuts, using a
metal spoon, then pour the mixture into the prepared tin.

3   Bake in the hot oven for 45–50 minutes, or until a
skewer inserted into the middle comes out with just a few
moist crumbs on it. Remove from the oven, and leave the
cake in the tin to cool for 10 minutes.

4   Remove the cake from the tin and serve warm with the
rich chocolate sauce.

150

Cakes & bakes

There
is nothing more
wonderful than the aroma
of freshly baked cakes and
biscuits. Baking really is a very
simple skill to master and requires
only a light touch and good-quality,
fresh ingredients. Here you will find
a fantastic selection of recipes,
for cakes, brownies, cookies,
squares, scones and
muffins.

Warm chocolate & nut torte

PREPARATION TIME 20 minutes   COOKING TIME 40–45 minutes

MAKES 1 x 23cm/9in torte

185g/6½oz butter, softened,
   plus extra for greasing
185g/6½oz/¾ cup plus 1 tbsp
   caster sugar
1 tsp vanilla essence
3 eggs, lightly beaten
185g/6½oz/1¾ cups ground
   almonds
100g/3½oz/¾ cup walnuts,
   roasted and finely chopped
4 tbsp plain flour
½ tsp baking powder
4 tbsp Marsala wine
1 recipe quantity Dark
   Chocolate Ganache
   (see page 196)

1   Preheat the oven to 170°C/325°F/gas 3. Grease a 23cm/9in spring-form cake tin with butter, and line the base with baking paper.

2   In a large bowl, beat the butter, sugar and vanilla essence together until light and creamy, using an electric hand mixer. Beat in the eggs, one at a time. In a clean bowl, mix together the nuts, flour and baking powder, using a wooden spoon. Fold into the butter mixture with the Marsala, then pour into the prepared tin.

3   Bake in the hot oven for 40–45 minutes, or until the torte is lightly browned and firm in the middle. Remove from the oven and leave the torte to cool in the tin for 10 minutes. Turn the torte out on to a wire rack, and leave to cool completely.

4   To ice the torte, use a palette knife to spread the dark chocolate ganache over the top.

Flourless chocolate & citrus cake

PREPARATION TIME 25 minutes   COOKING TIME 45–50 minutes

MAKES 1 x 23cm/9in cake

175g/6oz butter, melted and left to cool, plus extra for greasing
6 eggs, separated
200g/7oz/¾ cup plus 2 tbsp caster sugar
zest of 1 orange, finely grated
zest of 1 lemon, finely grated
125ml/4fl oz/½ cup orange juice
125g/4½oz/1¼ cups ground almonds
2 tbsp cocoa powder
250g/9oz dark chocolate, melted and left to cool
icing sugar, sifted, for dusting

1   Preheat the oven to 180°C/350°F/gas 4. Grease a deep 23cm/9in spring-form round cake tin with butter, and line the base with baking paper.

2   In a large bowl, beat the egg yolks, sugar, orange and lemon zest together until thick and pale, using an electric hand mixer. Stir in the melted butter and the orange juice. In a clean bowl, combine the ground almonds and cocoa, then fold into the egg mixture. In a clean bowl, whisk the egg whites to soft peaks, using clean attachments for the electric hand mixer, then pour in the melted chocolate and stir together. Fold into the cake mixture until just combined, using a metal spoon, then pour into the prepared tin.

3   Bake in the hot oven for 45–50 minutes, or until the cake is firm around the edges but still slightly soft in the middle. Remove from the oven and leave the cake in the tin to cool completely, then remove the cake from the tin and dust with icing sugar.

Easy fudge cake

PREPARATION TIME 15 minutes   COOKING TIME 25–30 minutes

MAKES 1 x 23cm/9in cake

75g/2¾oz butter, melted, plus extra for greasing
200g/7oz/1 cup plus 1 tbsp soft brown sugar
2 eggs, lightly beaten
1 tsp vanilla essence
140g/5oz/1¼ cups self-raising flour
2 tbsp cocoa powder
1 recipe quantity Creamy Chocolate Icing (see page 202)

1 Preheat the oven to 180°C/350°F/gas 4. Grease a 23cm/9in spring-form cake tin with butter, and line the base with baking paper.

2 In a large bowl, beat the butter and sugar together, using an electric hand mixer, then add the eggs and vanilla essence, beating until well combined. In another bowl, combine the flour and cocoa, then add to the sugar mixture with 125ml/4fl oz/½ cup hot water, stirring with a wooden spoon just until everything is moist. Pour into the prepared tin.

3 Bake in the hot oven for 25–30 minutes, or until a skewer inserted into the middle of the cake comes out clean. Remove from the oven and leave the cake in the tin to cool for 10 minutes, then turn out on to a wire rack to cool completely.

4 To ice the cake, use a palette knife to spread over the creamy chocolate icing.

Chocolate ricotta cake

PREPARATION TIME 20 minutes   COOKING TIME 30–35 minutes

MAKES 1 x 23cm/9in cake

150g/5½oz butter, softened,
    plus extra for greasing
100g/3½oz/⅓ cup plus
    4 tsp caster sugar
150g/5½oz dark chocolate,
    melted and left to cool
3 eggs, separated
250g/9oz ricotta cheese
100g/3½oz/1 cup ground
    almonds
2 tbsp plain flour
icing sugar, sifted, for dusting

1 Preheat the oven to 170°C/325°F/gas 4. Grease a
23cm/9in spring-form tin with butter, and line the base
with baking paper.

2 In a large bowl, beat the butter and sugar together
until light and fluffy, using an electric hand mixer. Add
the melted chocolate, egg yolks and ricotta, stirring with
a wooden spoon until just combined, then stir in the
ground almonds and flour. In a clean bowl, whisk the
egg whites to soft peaks, using clean attachments for the
electric hand mixer, then fold into the chocolate mixture.
Pour into the prepared tin.

3 Bake in the hot oven for 30–35 minutes until the
cake is just firm around the edges but still wobbly in the
middle. Remove from the oven and leave in the tin to
cool for 10–15 minutes, then remove the cake from the
tin and transfer to a serving plate. Dust with icing sugar
and serve warm.

Chocolate angel food cake

PREPARATION TIME 15 minutes   COOKING TIME 45–50 minutes

MAKES 1 x 21 x 10cm/8½ x 4in cake

6 eggs, separated
250ml/9fl oz/1 cup vegetable
   oil
150g/5½oz/1¼ cups drinking
   chocolate
280g/10oz/2¼ cups self-
   raising flour
400g/14oz/1½ cups plus
   4 tbsp caster sugar
icing sugar, sifted, for dusting

1   Preheat the oven to 150°C/300°F/gas 2. Place an
ungreased, loose-bottomed angel food cake tin on a baking
tray. (If you do not have an angel food cake tin, use a ring
tin of the same diameter, but make only half of the recipe.)
2   Place the egg yolks, oil, drinking chocolate, flour,
sugar and 250ml/9fl oz/1 cup water in a large bowl,
and mix on low speed with an electric hand mixer until
just combined. Then beat at the highest setting for 10
minutes. In a clean bowl, whisk the egg whites until stiff,
using clean attachments for the electric hand mixer,
then fold gently into the chocolate mixture using a metal
spoon. Pour into the prepared tin.
3   Bake in the warm oven for 45–50 minutes, or until
the cake is firm when touched. Remove from the oven
and turn the cake tin upside down on to a wire rack, then
leave the cake in the tin until it has cooled completely.
4   When cold, loosen the cake from the tin with a
sharp knife, turn out on to a serving plate and dust
with icing sugar.

Chocolate pear upside-down cake

PREPARATION TIME 20 minutes   COOKING TIME 30–35 minutes

MAKES 1 x 23cm/9In cake

200g/7oz butter, softened,
    plus extra for greasing
200g/7oz dark chocolate,
    broken into pieces
150g/5½oz/⅔ cup caster sugar
3 eggs, lightly beaten
1 tsp vanilla essence
100g/3½oz/¾ cup plus 1 tbsp
    self-raising flour
3 tbsp soft brown sugar
3 pears, ripe but firm, peeled,
    cored and sliced into
    quarters

1 Preheat the oven to 180°C/350°F/gas 4. Grease a 23cm/9in spring-form cake tin with butter, and line the base with baking paper.

2 In a small saucepan, combine the butter, chocolate and sugar over a low heat until just melted, stirring with a wooden spoon. Remove from the heat and set aside to cool completely. Stir in the eggs, vanilla essence and flour until just combined. Sprinkle the brown sugar over the base of the tin, arrange the pear quarters over the top in a spiral shape, and pour over the chocolate batter.

3 Bake in the hot oven for 25–30 minutes, or until a skewer inserted in the middle of the cake comes out with just a few moist crumbs on it. Remove from the oven and leave the cake in the tin to cool for 15 minutes, then turn out on to a wire rack to cool completely, pear side up.

White chocolate Sauternes cake

PREPARATION TIME 20 minutes   COOKING TIME 30–35 minutes

MAKES 1 x 23cm/9in cake

175g/6oz butter, softened,
  plus extra for greasing
225g/8oz/1 cup caster sugar
3 eggs, lightly beaten
125g/4½oz/1 cup plain flour
100g/3½oz/¾ cup plus 1 tbsp
  self-raising flour
125ml/4fl oz/½ cup milk
100ml/3½fl oz/⅓ cup
  Sauternes
200g/7oz white chocolate,
  melted and left to cool
1 recipe quantity White
  Chocolate Frosting
  (see page 201)

1   Preheat the oven to 180°C/350°F/gas 4. Grease a 23cm/9in spring-form cake tin with butter, and line the base with baking paper.

2   In a large bowl, beat the butter and sugar together until light and creamy, using an electric hand mixer, then gradually beat in the eggs until smooth. In a clean bowl, combine the flours using a wooden spoon, then fold into the butter mixture with the milk and half of the Sauternes, using a metal spoon. Stir in the melted chocolate, and pour the mixture into the prepared tin.

3   Bake in the hot oven for 30–35 minutes, or until a skewer inserted into the middle of the cake comes out clean. Remove from the oven and leave the cake in the tin to cool for 10 minutes, then turn out on to a wire rack to cool completely. Pierce a few holes in the top of the cake with a skewer, then drizzle over the remaining Sauternes. Leave the cake to cool completely.

4   To ice the cake, use a palette knife to spread over the white chocolate frosting.

Chocolate cream roll with strawberries

PREPARATION TIME 35 minutes   COOKING TIME 10–12 minutes

MAKES 1 x cream roll

butter, for greasing

4 eggs, separated

200g/7oz/¾ cup plus 2 tbsp caster sugar, plus 2 tbsp for sprinkling

75g/2¾oz dark or milk chocolate, grated

75g/2¾oz/½ cup plus 1 tbsp self-raising flour

1 recipe quantity Chocolate Chantilly Cream (see page 194)

150g/5½oz/1 cup strawberries, hulled and sliced

1   Preheat the oven to 180°C/350°F/gas 4. Grease a 33 x 23cm/13 x 9in Swiss roll tin with butter, and line the base and sides with baking paper.

2   In a large bowl, beat the egg yolks and half the sugar together until thick and creamy, using an electric hand mixer. Stir in 2 tbsp water, the grated chocolate and flour, using a wooden spoon. In a clean bowl, whisk the egg whites to soft peaks, using clean attachments for the electric hand mixer, then continue whisking, gradually adding the remaining sugar, until thick and shiny. Fold into the chocolate mixture until just combined, using a metal spoon. Pour the mixture into the prepared tin and spread evenly, using a palette knife.

3   Bake in the hot oven for 10–12 minutes, or until just firm. Remove from the oven and turn out on to a large sheet of baking paper that has been sprinkled with sugar. Remove the lining paper, then, using the baking paper to help you, roll up from a short side, enclosing the paper in the cake. Leave to cool completely.

4   When cool, unroll the cake carefully, spread with the chocolate Chantilly cream and scatter over the strawberries. Re-roll, transfer to a serving plate and refrigerate until ready to serve.

Chocolate & almond marble cake

PREPARATION TIME 20 minutes   COOKING TIME 18–20 minutes

MAKES 1 x 23cm/9in cake

170g/6oz butter, softened, plus extra for greasing
170g/6oz/¾ cup caster sugar
1 egg, lightly beaten
1 tsp vanilla essence
100g/3½oz/1 cup ground almonds
100g/3½oz/¾ cup plus 1 tbsp self-raising flour
60ml/2fl oz/¼ cup milk
150g/5½oz milk chocolate, melted and left to cool
1 recipe quantity Dark Chocolate Ganache (see page 196)

1   Preheat the oven to 180°C/350°F/gas 4. Grease an 23cm/9in square cake tin with butter, and line the base with baking paper.

2   In a large bowl, beat the butter and sugar together until light and fluffy, using an electric hand mixer. Gradually beat in the egg and vanilla essence until well combined. In a clean bowl, mix together the almonds and flour, using a wooden spoon, then gently fold into the butter mixture with the milk, using a metal spoon. Place half of the cake mixture into the prepared tin. Fold the melted chocolate into the remaining mixture and pour into the tin. Gently draw a fork through the mix to create a swirled effect.

3   Bake in the hot oven for 18–20 minutes, or until the cake is just firm. Remove from the oven and leave the cake in the tin to cool for 10 minutes, then turn out on to a wire rack to cool completely.

4   To ice the cake, use a palette knife to spread over the chocolate ganache.

Orange loaf cake with chocolate chips

PREPARATION TIME 20 minutes   COOKING TIME 40–45 minutes
MAKES 1 x 24 x 12cm/9 x 4½in loaf cake

175g/6oz butter, softened,
    plus extra for greasing
175g/6oz/¾ cup caster sugar
2 eggs, lightly beaten
175g/6oz/1⅓ cups plus 1 tbsp
    self-raising flour
100g/3½oz dark or milk
    chocolate chips
zest of 1 orange, grated,
    plus juice
1 tbsp milk
1 recipe quantity Chocolate
    Buttercream (see page 194)

1 Preheat the oven to 180°C/350°F/gas 4. Grease a 24 x 12cm/9 x 4½in loaf tin with butter, and line the base with baking paper.

2 In a large bowl, beat the butter and sugar together until light and fluffy, using an electric hand mixer, then gradually beat in the eggs. Fold in the flour, chocolate chips, orange zest and milk until just combined, and pour into the prepared tin.

3 Bake in the hot oven for 40–45 minutes, or until a skewer inserted into the centre comes out with just a few moist crumbs on it. Remove from the oven.

4 Pierce the top of the cake in 3 or 4 places with the skewer and brush over the orange juice. Cool for 10 minutes, then turn out on to a wire rack and top with chocolate buttercream.

Chocolate banana bread

PREPARATION TIME 20 minutes   COOKING TIME 50–55 minutes

MAKES 1 x 24 x 12cm/9 x 4½in loaf

125g/4½oz butter, softened,
   plus extra for greasing and
   to serve
125g/4½oz/⅔ cup soft brown
   sugar
2 eggs, lightly beaten
150g/5½oz dark chocolate,
   melted and left to cool
3 ripe bananas, mashed
1 tsp vanilla essence
200g/7oz/1⅔ cups plus 1 tbsp
   self-raising flour

1 Preheat the oven to 180°C/350°F/gas 4. Grease a 24 x 12cm/9 x 4½in loaf tin with butter, and line the base with baking paper.

2 In a large bowl, beat the butter and sugar together until light and fluffy, using an electric hand mixer. Add the eggs, beating well, then stir in the melted chocolate, bananas, vanilla essence and flour until just combined, using a wooden spoon. Spoon into the prepared tin.

3 Bake in the hot oven for 50–55 minutes, or until a skewer inserted into the middle of the cake comes out with just a few crumbs clinging to it. Remove from the oven and leave the cake in the tin to cool for 10 minutes, then turn out on to a wire rack to cool completely. Serve with butter for spreading.

Pear, pistachio & chocolate loaf cake

PREPARATION TIME 30 minutes   COOKING TIME 55–60 minutes

MAKES 1 x 24 x 12cm/9 x 4½in loaf cake

150g/5½oz butter, softened,
plus extra for greasing
150g/5½oz/⅔ cup caster sugar
3 eggs, lightly beaten
1 tsp vanilla essence
200g/7oz dark chocolate,
finely chopped
1 pear, peeled, cored and
diced
60g/2¼oz/⅓ cup pistachio nuts
150g/5½oz/1 cup plus 2 tbsp
self-raising flour

1   Preheat the oven to 180°C/350°F/gas 4. Grease a 24 x 12cm/9 x 4½in loaf tin with butter.

2   In a large bowl, beat the butter and sugar together until light and fluffy, using an electric hand mixer. Add the eggs one at a time, whisking well in between, then add the vanilla essence. Fold in the chocolate, pear, pistachio nuts and flour until just combined, using a wooden spoon. Pour into the prepared tin.

3   Bake in the hot oven for 55–60 minutes, or until a skewer inserted into the middle of the cake comes out clean. Remove from the oven and leave the cake in the tin to cool for 10 minutes, then turn out on to a wire rack to cool completely.

Chocolate ginger cake

PREPARATION TIME 25 minutes   COOKING TIME 35–40 minutes

MAKES 1 x 23cm/9in cake

150g/5½oz butter, softened,
    plus extra for greasing
150g/5½oz/¾ cup plus 1 tbsp
    soft brown sugar
2 eggs, lightly beaten
2 tbsp chopped stem ginger
1 tbsp clear honey
100g/3½oz dark chocolate,
    melted and left to cool
150g/5½oz/1 cup plus 2 tbsp
    self-raising flour
2 tsp ground ginger
1 tbsp dark rum
1 recipe quantity Chocolate
    Rum Frosting (see page 199)

1   Preheat the oven to 180°C/350°F/gas 4. Grease a 23cm/9in square cake tin with butter, and line the base with baking paper.

2   In a large bowl, beat the butter and sugar together until light and fluffy, using an electric hand mixer, then add the eggs and beat until smooth. Stir in the chopped ginger, honey and melted chocolate until just combined, using a wooden spoon. Sift the flour and ground ginger together and fold into the cake mixture with the rum, using a metal spoon. Spoon into the prepared tin.

3   Bake in the hot oven for 35–40 minutes, or until the cake is just firm in the middle. Remove from the oven and leave the cake in the tin to cool for 10 minutes, then turn out on to a wire rack to cool completely.

4   To ice the cake, use a palette knife to spread over the chocolate rum frosting.

Chocolate madeleines

PREPARATION TIME 15 minutes   COOKING TIME 15–17 minutes

MAKES 12–14 madeleines

100g/3½oz butter, chopped,
   plus extra for greasing
75g/2¾oz dark chocolate,
   broken into pieces
75g/2¾oz/½ cup plus 1 tbsp
   plain flour
½ tsp baking powder
pinch salt
2 eggs
100g/3½oz/⅓ cup plus 4 tsp
   caster sugar
icing sugar, sifted, for dusting

1 Preheat the oven to 180°C/350°F/gas 4. Grease a 12-hole madeleine tin with butter.

2 In a small saucepan, heat the butter and chocolate together over a low heat until just melted, then set aside to cool. Sift the flour and baking powder into a bowl, and add the salt. In a large bowl, beat the eggs and sugar together until the mixture is light in colour, using an electric hand mixer, then whisk in the chocolate mixture. Using a metal spoon, gently fold in the flour mix, then divide the mixture between the holes in the prepared tin, taking care not to overfill.

3 Bake in the hot oven for 10–12 minutes until the cakes are firm to the touch. Remove from the oven and leave the madeleines in the tin to cool for 10 minutes, then turn out on to a wire rack to cool completely and dust with icing sugar.

Dark & white chocolate brownies

PREPARATION TIME 25 minutes   COOKING TIME 20–25 minutes

MAKES 12 brownies

175g/6oz butter, chopped,
  plus extra for greasing
2 tbsp cocoa powder
300g/10½oz/1⅓ cups caster
  sugar
2 eggs, lightly beaten
1 tsp vanilla essence
150g/5½oz/1 cup plus 2 tbsp
  plain flour
60g/2¼oz white chocolate
  chips
60g/2¼oz dark chocolate
  chips
60g/2¼oz/⅔ cup walnuts,
  roughly chopped

1   Preheat the oven to 180°C/350°F/gas 4. Grease a shallow 23cm/9in square tin with butter and line the base with baking paper, leaving some hanging over the edges to make removing the brownies easier.

2   In a large saucepan, heat the butter with the cocoa and sugar over a low heat until just melted, remove from the heat and set aside to cool. When cool, add the remaining ingredients, and stir with a wooden spoon until just combined. Pour into the prepared tin.

3   Bake in the hot oven for 15–20 minutes, or until the brownie is firm around the edges and still slightly soft in the middle. Remove from the oven and leave in the tin to cool completely, then cut into 12 squares.

Cappuccino brownies

PREPARATION TIME 20 minutes   COOKING TIME 20–25 minutes

MAKES 12 brownies

175g/6oz butter, chopped,
plus extra for greasing
2 tbsp cocoa powder
2 tsp instant coffee granules
250g/9oz/1 cup plus 4 tsp
caster sugar
2 eggs, lightly beaten
1 tsp vanilla essence
150g/5½oz/1 cup plus 2 tbsp
plain flour
1 recipe quantity White
Chocolate Frosting (see
page 201)
1 tbsp cocoa powder, sifted

1   Preheat the oven to 180°C/350°F/gas 4. Grease a shallow 23cm/9in square tin with butter and line the base with baking paper, leaving some hanging over the edges to make removing the brownies easier.

2   In a small saucepan, heat the butter with the cocoa, coffee and sugar over a low heat until just melted, remove from the heat and set aside to cool. When cool, add the eggs, vanilla essence and flour, and stir with a wooden spoon until just combined. Pour into the prepared tin.

3   Bake in the hot oven for 15–20 minutes, or until the brownie is firm around the edges and still slightly soft in the middle. Remove from the oven and leave in the tin to cool completely.

4   To ice the brownie, use a palette knife to spread the white chocolate frosting over the top. Sprinkle with the cocoa, then cut into 12 squares.

White chocolate, lime & coconut cup cakes

PREPARATION TIME 20 minutes   COOKING TIME 18–20 minutes
MAKES 12 cup cakes

150g/5½oz/1 cup plus 2 tbsp
   self-raising flour
3 tbsp plus 1 tsp caster sugar
50g/1¾oz butter, melted
1 egg, lightly beaten
100ml/3½fl oz/⅓ cup milk
1 tsp vanilla essence
juice and zest of 1 lime
100g/3½oz white chocolate,
   broken into pieces
45g/1½oz/½ cup desiccated
   coconut
1 recipe quantity White
   Chocolate Frosting (see
   page 201)

1   Preheat the oven to 180°C/350°F/gas 4. Place 12 paper cake cases into the holes of a 12-hole muffin tin.
2   In a large bowl, combine the flour and sugar, and make a well in the middle. Mix together the butter, egg, milk, vanilla essence, lime juice and zest, using a wooden spoon, and stir into the flour mixture until just combined. Stir in the white chocolate and coconut, then use a dessertspoon to divide the mixture evenly between the cake cases.
3   Bake in the hot oven for 18–20 minutes, or until the cakes are firm to the touch. Remove from the oven and transfer to wire racks to cool completely.
4   To ice the cakes, use a palette knife to spread over the white chocolate frosting.

Chocolate cup cakes

PREPARATION TIME 20 minutes   COOKING TIME 12–15 minutes

MAKES 12 cup cakes

125g/4½oz butter, softened
125g/4½oz/½ cup plus 2 tsp
   caster sugar
2 eggs, lightly beaten
125g/4½oz/1 cup self-raising
   flour
3 tbsp cocoa powder
2 tbsp milk
½ tsp vanilla essence
1 recipe quantity Creamy
   Chocolate Icing (see
   page 202)

1 Preheat the oven to 180°C/350°F/gas 4. Place 12 paper cake cases into the holes of a 12-hole muffin tin.

2 In a large bowl, beat the butter and sugar until light and creamy, using an electric hand mixer, then gradually whisk in the eggs until well blended. In a clean bowl, sift the flour and cocoa together, then fold into the butter mixture, using a metal spoon, along with the milk and vanilla essence. Divide the mixture evenly between the cake cases.

3 Bake in the hot oven for 12–15 minutes, or until the cakes are firm to the touch. Remove from the oven and transfer to wire racks to cool completely.

4 To ice the cakes, use a palette knife to spread over the creamy chocolate icing.

Blondies

PREPARATION TIME 20 minutes   COOKING TIME 25–30 minutes

MAKES 12 blondies

100g/3½oz butter, chopped, plus extra for greasing
125g/4½oz white chocolate, broken into pieces
200g/7oz/¾ cup plus 2 tbsp caster sugar
3 eggs, lightly beaten
1 tsp vanilla essence
100g/3½oz/¾ cup hazelnuts, skinned and chopped
100g/3½oz white chocolate chips
175g/6oz/1⅓ cups plus 1 tbsp plain flour

1   Preheat the oven to 180°C/350°F/gas 4. Grease a shallow 23cm/9in square tin with butter, and line the base with baking paper.

2   In a small saucepan, heat the butter and chocolate together over a low heat until the chocolate has just melted, then remove from the heat and stir gently until smooth. In a large bowl, combine the sugar and eggs, then stir in the chocolate mixture, vanilla essence, hazelnuts, chocolate chips and flour, using a wooden spoon. Pour into the prepared tin.

3   Bake in the hot oven for 20–25 minutes, or until the cake is firm around the edges but still moist in the middle. Remove from the oven, and leave the cake in the tin to cool completely. Remove the cake from the tin and cut into 12 squares.

Chocolate almond squares

PREPARATION TIME 15 minutes   COOKING TIME 20–25 minutes

MAKES 16 squares

100g/3½oz butter, softened,
   plus extra for greasing
5 tbsp caster sugar
4 eggs, separated
100g/3½oz dark chocolate,
   grated
185g/6½oz/1¾ cups ground
   almonds
4 tbsp plain flour
1 tbsp brandy
1 recipe quantity Shiny
   Chocolate Icing (see
   page 202)

1   Preheat the oven to 180°C/350°F/gas 4. Grease a shallow 23cm/9in square tin with butter, then line the base with baking paper.

2   In a large bowl, mix together the butter, sugar, egg yolks, chocolate, ground almonds, flour and brandy, using a wooden spoon. In a clean bowl, whisk the egg whites to soft peaks, using an electric hand mixer, then fold into the chocolate mixture, using a metal spoon. Pour into the prepared tin.

3   Bake in the hot oven for 20–25 minutes, or until the cake is firm and lightly browned. Remove from the oven and leave the cake to cool completely in the tin.

4   To ice, use a palette knife to spread over the shiny chocolate icing, then cut into 16 squares.

White chocolate fruit & nut slice

PREPARATION TIME 20 minutes   COOKING TIME 35–40 minutes

MAKES 16 slices

butter, for greasing
100g/3½oz/1 cup flaked
    almonds
200g/7oz/2 cups walnuts,
    chopped
150g/5½oz/1⅔ cups
    desiccated coconut
150g/5½oz/¾ cup dried
    apricots, chopped
150g/5½oz/1 cup plus 2 tbsp
    raisins
2 tbsp plus 1 tsp rice flour
25g/1oz/¼ cup ground
    almonds
150g/5½oz/½ cup apricot jam
125ml/4fl oz/½ cup honey
250g/9oz white chocolate,
    melted and left to cool

1   Preheat the oven to 170°C/325°F/gas 3. Grease a shallow 30 x 22cm/12 x 8in tin with butter, and line with baking paper.

2   In a large bowl, mix the almonds, walnuts, coconut, apricots, raisins, flour and ground almonds together. In a small saucepan, gently warm the jam and honey together over a low heat until melted. Pour the jam and honey mixture into the fruit mixture, stir well to combine, then pour into the prepared tin.

3   Bake in the hot oven for 30–35 minutes, or until the slice is lightly browned. Remove from the oven, and leave the slice in the baking tray to cool completely before spreading the melted chocolate over the top. Leave to set before cutting into 16 slices.

Chocolate flapjacks

PREPARATION TIME 20 minutes   COOKING TIME 15–20 minutes

MAKES 18 flapjacks

350g/12oz butter, chopped,
    plus extra for greasing
3 tbsp golden syrup
175g/6oz/¾ cup plus 3 tbsp
    soft brown sugar
100g/3½oz/⅓ cup plus 4 tsp
    caster sugar
5 tbsp cocoa powder
350g/12oz/3½ cups rolled oats

1 Preheat the oven to 150°C/300°F/gas 2. Grease a shallow 23cm/9in square cake tin with butter, and line the base with baking paper.

2 In a small saucepan, melt the butter with the golden syrup, over a low heat. Remove from the heat and set aside. In a large bowl, mix together both sugars, cocoa and rolled oats, using a wooden spoon, then pour the butter mixture into the bowl. Stir until well combined then press the mixture into the prepared tin.

3 Bake in the warm oven for 15–20 minutes, or until just firm in the middle. Remove from the oven, and leave in the tin to cool completely before cutting into 18 pieces.

Cranberry & white chocolate scones

PREPARATION TIME 20 minutes   COOKING TIME 15–20 minutes

MAKES 6 large scones

75g/2¾oz butter, chilled and chopped, plus extra for greasing and to serve

250g/9oz/2 cups self-raising flour

3 tbsp plus 1 tsp caster sugar

75g/2¾oz white chocolate chips

100g/3½oz/¾ cup plus 1 tbsp dried cranberries

6 tbsp milk, plus extra for brushing

1 egg, lightly beaten

1   Preheat the oven to 190°C/375°F/gas 5. Grease a large baking tray with butter.

2   Place the flour and sugar in a large bowl, and, working lightly, rub in the butter with your fingertips until the mixture resembles breadcrumbs. Stir in the chocolate chips and cranberries, using a wooden spoon. In a small bowl, beat together the milk and egg. Add the milk mixture to the flour mixture until it forms a soft dough, using a rounded knife and a cutting motion.

3   Turn the dough out on to a lightly floured board and pat it out until it is around 2.5cm/1in thick. Cut out 6 circles using a scone cutter, and place on the prepared tray. Brush the tops with a little extra milk, using a pastry brush.

4   Bake in the hot oven for 15–20 minutes, or until the scones are golden brown. Remove from the oven and transfer to a wire rack to cool completely, then transfer to a serving plate and serve warm or cold with butter.

White chocolate & blueberry muffins

PREPARATION TIME 15 minutes   COOKING TIME 15–20 minutes

MAKES 12 muffins

125g/4½oz butter, melted,
  plus extra for greasing
250g/9oz/2 cups self-raising
  flour
100g/3½oz/⅓ cup plus
  4 tsp caster sugar
125g/4½oz white chocolate,
  broken into pieces
1 egg, lightly beaten
125ml/4fl oz/½ cup milk
1 tsp vanilla essence
150g/5½oz/1 cup blueberries

1 Preheat the oven to 190°C/375°F/gas 5. Grease a 12-hole muffin tin with butter.

2 In a large bowl, mix all the ingredients together until just combined, using a wooden spoon. Divide the mixture evenly between the prepared tin holes.

3 Bake in the hot oven for 15–20 minutes until the muffins have risen and are golden brown. Remove from the oven and leave the muffins in the tin to cool for 5-10 minutes, then remove the muffins from the tin and transfer to a wire rack to cool completely.

Double chocolate muffins

PREPARATION TIME 15 minutes   COOKING TIME 20–25 minutes

MAKES 12 muffins

125g/4½oz butter, melted,
    plus extra for greasing
375g/13oz/3 cups self-raising
    flour
3 tbsp cocoa powder
175g/6oz/¾ cup caster sugar
2 eggs, lightly beaten
125g/4½oz dark or milk
    chocolate chips
250ml/9fl oz/1 cup milk

1   Preheat the oven to 190°C/375°F/gas 5. Grease a 12-hole muffin tin with butter.

2   In a large bowl, mix together all the ingredients until just combined, using a wooden spoon. Divide the mixture evenly between the prepared tin holes.

3   Bake in the hot oven for 20–25 minutes until the muffins have risen and are golden brown. Remove from the oven and leave in the tin to cool for 5–10 minutes, then remove from the tin and transfer to a wire rack to cool completely.

Chocolate cherry macaroons

PREPARATION TIME 10 minutes, plus chilling   COOKING TIME 18–20 minutes

MAKES 20 macaroons

butter, for greasing
150g/5½oz/1⅔ cups
  desiccated coconut
200ml/7fl oz/¾ cup coconut
  cream
2 tbsp cocoa powder
100g/3½oz/¾ cup plus 1 tbsp
  icing sugar
2 large egg whites
100g/3½oz/½ cup glacé
  cherries, finely chopped

1   Preheat the oven to 170°C/325°F/gas 3. Line 2 large baking trays with baking paper.

2   In a large bowl, mix all of the ingredients until well combined, using a wooden spoon. Refrigerate the mixture for 30 minutes. Place 20 heaped teaspoonfuls of the mixture on the prepared baking tray, leaving approximately 5cm/2in between them to allow for spreading.

3   Bake in the hot oven for 18–20 minutes, or until the macaroons look just firm. (You may need to cook them in batches.) Remove the macaroons from the oven and leave to cool on the trays for 5 minutes before transferring to a wire rack to cool completely.

Chocolate melting moments

PREPARATION TIME 20 minutes   COOKING TIME 8–10 minutes

MAKES 20 biscuits

125g/4½oz butter, softened,
  plus extra for greasing
4 tbsp icing sugar, plus extra,
  sifted, for dusting
125g/4½oz/1 cup plain flour
3 tbsp cocoa powder

1   Preheat the oven to 180°C/350°F/gas 4. Grease 2 large baking trays with butter.

2   In a large bowl, mix the butter and sugar together, using a wooden spoon, until light and fluffy. In a clean bowl, combine the flour and cocoa, then stir into the butter mixture until just combined (the mixture will be soft). Place a little flour on your hands, and roll the mixture into 20 balls. Place 10 balls of dough on each baking tray, leaving approximately 5cm/2in between them to allow for spreading, and press the top of each biscuit down with a lightly floured fork.

3   Bake in the hot oven for 8–10 minutes, or until the biscuits are firm. (You may need to cook them in batches.) Remove the melting moments from the oven and leave to cool on the trays for 5 minutes before transferring to a wire rack to cool completely. Dust with the extra sugar.

Orange chocolate-chip biscuits

PREPARATION TIME 20 minutes   COOKING TIME 10–12 minutes

MAKES 24 biscuits

125g/4½oz butter, softened,
   plus extra for greasing
1 tsp vanilla essence
75g/2¾oz/⅓ cup plus 1 tbsp
   soft brown sugar
5 tbsp caster sugar
1 egg, lightly beaten
185g/6½oz/1⅓ cups plus
   2 tbsp plain flour
1 tsp cardamom
1 tsp cinnamon
zest of 1 orange, grated
200g/7oz orange-flavoured
   chocolate, broken into
   pieces

1 Preheat the oven to 180°C/350°F/gas 4. Grease 2 large baking trays with butter.

2 In a large bowl, beat together the butter, vanilla essence, brown sugar and caster sugar until light and creamy, using an electric hand mixer. Add the egg until well combined, then stir in the remaining ingredients. Place 24 tablespoonfuls of the mixture on the prepared baking trays, leaving approximately 5cm/2in between them to allow for spreading.

3 Bake in the hot oven for 10–12 minutes, or until the biscuits are dark brown. (You may need to cook them in batches.) Remove the biscuits from the oven and transfer to wire racks to cool completely.

Chocolate & pistachio biscotti

PREPARATION TIME 35 minutes   COOKING TIME 50–65 minutes

MAKES approximately 20 biscotti

125g/4½oz/½ cup plus 2 tsp
  caster sugar
1 egg
125g/4½oz/1 cup plain flour
2 tbsp cocoa powder
½ tsp baking powder
50g/1¾oz/¾ cup pistachio
  nuts, roughly chopped

1 Preheat the oven to 170°C/325°F/gas 3. Line a large baking tray with baking paper.

2 In a large bowl, beat the sugar and egg together until pale and thick, using an electric hand mixer. In a separate bowl, combine the remaining ingredients, using a metal spoon, and fold into the egg mixture to form a dough. Remove the dough from the bowl and gently knead it on a lightly floured surface for about 30 seconds. Form a log about 18 x 5cm/7 x 2in in size, and place on the prepared baking tray.

3 Bake in the hot oven for 20–25 minutes, or until the dough is firm to the touch. Remove from the oven, turning the temperature down to 140°C/275°F/gas 1, and leave to cool completely. When the dough is cold, cut it into approximately 20 slices around 5mm/¼in thick, using a serrated knife.

4 Place the biscotti slices on a fresh baking tray, and bake them in the warm oven for 30–40 minutes, turning once, until they are very dry. Remove the biscotti from the oven and leave to cool completely.

Truffle dough cookies

PREPARATION TIME 15 minutes, plus chilling   COOKING TIME 10–12 minutes

MAKES 20 cookies

100g/3½oz/⅓ cup plus 4 tsp
   caster sugar
75g/2¾oz/½ cup plus 1 tbsp
   self-raising flour
3 tbsp cocoa powder
pinch salt
25g/1oz butter, chopped
1 egg, lightly beaten
1 tsp vanilla essence
icing sugar, sifted, for rolling
   and dusting

1   Line a large baking tray with baking paper.

2   Place the sugar, flour, cocoa, salt and butter in the bowl of a food processor, and pulse for 30 seconds. Add the egg and vanilla essence, and pulse for 15 seconds more, or until the mixture forms a dough. Remove the dough from the processor and refrigerate for 30 minutes. Preheat the oven to 180°C/350°F/gas 4.

3   Roll the dough into 20 balls about the size of a walnut, then roll these balls in icing sugar and place on the prepared tray, leaving approximately 10cm/4in between them to allow for spreading.

4   Bake in the hot oven for 10–12 minutes until the cookies are just set. (You may need to cook them in batches.) Remove the cookies from the oven and transfer to a wire rack to cool completely. Dust with icing sugar.

Hazelnut thumbprints

PREPARATION TIME 20 minutes   COOKING TIME 10–12 minutes

MAKES 24 biscuits

125g/4½oz butter, softened,
   plus extra for greasing
125g/4½oz/½ cup plus 2 tsp
   caster sugar
1 egg, lightly beaten
75g/2¾oz/½ cup plus 1 tbsp
   plain flour
75g/2¾oz/½ cup plus 1 tbsp
   self-raising flour
2 tbsp cocoa powder
150g/5½oz chocolate hazelnut
   spread
icing sugar, sifted, for dusting

1   Preheat the oven to 180°C/350°F/gas 4. Grease 2 large baking trays with butter.

2   In a large bowl, beat the butter and sugar together until pale and creamy, using an electric hand mixer, then add the egg, beating well to combine. In a separate bowl, mix together both flours and the cocoa, using a wooden spoon, and stir into the butter mixture to form a dough.

3   Roll into 24 balls about the size of a walnut, and place on the prepared trays, leaving approximately 5cm/2in between them to allow for spreading. Push the middle of each ball of dough down with your thumb to create an indent, then place a teaspoonful of the chocolate hazelnut spread into each indented hole.

4   Bake in the hot oven for 10–12 minutes, or until the biscuits are firm. (You may need to cook them in batches.) Remove the thumbprints from the oven and leave to cool on the trays for 10 minutes before transferring to a wire rack to cool completely. Dust with icing sugar.

150

DEBERRY

Pastries & puddings

In this chapter
you will find a range
of hot and cold puddings
and tarts that make the perfect
ending for any occasion. There is
something for everyone, with recipes
such as Chocolate Crèmes Brûlées
and Pain-au-chocolat Pudding
providing delicious variations
on traditional comfort-food
family favourites.

Chocolate Scotch pancakes

PREPARATION TIME 10 minutes   COOKING TIME 15 minutes

MAKES approximately 12 mini pancakes

250g/9oz/2 cups self-raising
  flour
1 tbsp cocoa powder
100g/3½oz/⅓ cup plus 4 tsp
  caster sugar
250ml/9fl oz/1 cup milk
1 egg, lightly beaten
butter, melted, for cooking
  pancakes
icing sugar, sifted, for dusting

1   Sift the flour and cocoa into a large bowl, mix in the sugar, and make a well in the middle of the mixture. In a small bowl, whisk the milk and egg together with a hand whisk, and pour into the well. Stir to form a smooth batter with a wooden spoon.

2   Heat a non-stick frying pan over a medium heat and brush with melted butter. Pour in the batter to make rounds of 9cm/3½in. Cook for 1–2 minutes, or until the top of each pancake begins to show small bubbles, then turn over with a spatula and cook on the second side for 30 seconds more. Remove from the pan and repeat until all the pancake batter has been used.

3   Transfer the pancakes to plates, dust with icing sugar and serve warm.

Pear clafoutis with chocolate

PREPARATION TIME 25 minutes   COOKING TIME 20–25 minutes

75g/2¾oz butter, softened,
  plus extra for greasing
100g/3½oz/⅓ cup plus 4 tsp
  caster sugar
2 eggs, lightly beaten
125g/4½oz/1 cup self-raising
  flour
75g/2¾oz/¾ cup ground
  almonds
125ml/4fl oz/½ cup milk
100g/3½oz dark chocolate,
  melted and left to cool
3 pears, ripe but not soft,
  peeled, quartered and cored
pouring cream, to serve
  (optional)

1   Preheat the oven to 180°C/350°F/gas 4. Grease a
1.5-litre/52fl oz/6-cup capacity ovenproof dish with butter.
2   In a large bowl, cream the butter and sugar together,
using an electric hand mixer, then beat in the eggs, a little
at a time. Combine the flour and ground almonds and
fold into the butter mixture with the milk and melted
chocolate to make a batter. Scatter the pears in the bottom
of the baking dish and pour over the batter mixture.
3   Bake in the hot oven for 20–25 minutes; the middle
should still be soft. Remove from the oven and leave
the clafoutis to cool slightly, before serving with cream,
if wanted.

127

Mocha pots with ricotta & coffee liqueur

PREPARATION TIME 25 minutes, plus chilling   COOKING TIME 5 minutes

275ml/9½fl oz/1 cup plus
   2 tbsp double cream
50g/1¾oz dark chocolate,
   broken into pieces
350g/12oz ricotta cheese
100g/3½oz/¾ cup plus 1 tbsp
   icing sugar
2 tbsp coffee liqueur
1 tbsp coffee beans, freshly
   ground

1   In a small saucepan, heat 150ml/5fl oz/⅔ cup of the cream over a low heat until just simmering, then remove from the heat and add the chocolate. Stir until smooth, using a metal spoon, and pour into a clean bowl to cool.

2   Place the ricotta, icing sugar, liqueur and coffee beans in the bowl of a food processor and process until smooth. Add the remaining cream and process briefly until all the ingredients are just combined.

3   Divide the ricotta mixture evenly between 4 glasses. Spoon 1 tbsp of the chocolate mixture on top of the ricotta mixture in each glass and refrigerate for 30–40 minutes until just firm.

Chocolate crèmes brûlées

PREPARATION TIME 15 minutes, plus chilling   COOKING TIME 40–45 minutes

600ml/21fl oz/2½ cups double cream
75g/2¾oz dark chocolate, broken into pieces
1 tsp vanilla essence
6 egg yolks
3 tbsp caster sugar
85g/3oz/⅓ cup soft brown sugar

1 Preheat the oven to 130°C/250°F/gas ½.

2 In a small saucepan, heat the cream and chocolate together over a low heat until the chocolate has just melted. In a large bowl, beat the vanilla essence, egg yolks and caster sugar together, using a hand whisk, then whisk in the heated cream mixture, combining well.

3 Divide the mixture evenly between 4 x 150ml/5fl oz/⅓ cup capacity ovenproof ramekins or other pots. Place the ramekins in a bain marie (see page 10) and bake in the warm oven for 35–40 minutes, or until the custards are just set.

4 Remove the dish from the oven and take the ramekins out of the dish using tongs, then leave to cool for 30 minutes before refrigerating overnight.

5 Remove from the refrigerator. Sprinkle the brown sugar over the tops of the custards and place under a very hot grill until the sugar melts and caramelizes (or use a domestic blowtorch). Serve immediately.

Chocolate mud pastries

PREPARATION TIME 20 minutes   COOKING TIME 20–25 minutes

MAKES 12 pastries

375g/13oz packet ready-rolled
   puff pastry
75g/2¾oz dark chocolate,
   broken into pieces
25g/1oz butter, chopped
5 tbsp caster sugar
1 egg, lightly beaten
1 tsp vanilla essence
1 tbsp plain flour
icing sugar, sifted, for dusting

1   Preheat the oven to 200°C/400°F/gas 6.

2   Cut the pastry into 12 squares of approximately 10cm/4in, which will roughly fit the holes of a 12-hole muffin tin with around 1cm/½in extra. Gently ease each pastry square into a hole without stretching it, and refrigerate while preparing the filling.

3   In a small saucepan, heat the chocolate and butter over a low heat, and stir until just melted. Remove from the heat and set aside to cool for 10 minutes, then stir in the sugar, egg, vanilla essence and flour. Spoon 1–2 tbsp of the chocolate mixture into the middle of each pastry cup, taking care not to overfill.

4   Bake in the hot oven for 15–20 minutes, or until the pastry is golden and the filling has puffed up. Remove from the oven and leave the pastries in the tins for 5 minutes, then transfer to a wire rack to cool completely. Dust the pastries with icing sugar.

Chocolate self-saucing pudding

PREPARATION TIME 15 minutes   COOKING TIME 20–25 minutes

75g/2¾oz butter, plus extra
    for greasing
150g/5½oz/1 cup plus 2 tbsp
    self-raising flour
2 tbsp cocoa powder
100g/3½oz/⅓ cup plus 4 tsp
    caster sugar
125ml/4fl oz/½ cup milk
1 tsp vanilla essence
1 egg, lightly beaten

For the topping
100g/3½oz/½ cup soft brown
    sugar
2 tbsp cocoa powder

1   Preheat the oven to 180°C/350°F/gas 4. Grease a
1.5-litre/52fl oz/6-cup capacity ovenproof dish with butter.
2   In a medium-sized bowl, combine the flour, cocoa
and sugar. In a small saucepan, heat the butter, milk and
vanilla essence over a low heat until the butter has just
melted, then set aside to cool for 5 minutes. Whisk in
the egg, using a hand whisk, then stir all of the liquid
ingredients into the dry ingredients to combine. Pour
the mixture into the prepared ovenproof dish.
3   For the topping, combine the brown sugar with the
cocoa in a bowl, then sprinkle over the chocolate mixture
in the dish. Pour over 300ml/10½fl oz/1¼ cups boiling
water. Bake in the hot oven for 15–20 minutes, or until
the pudding is firm but still slightly soft in the middle.
4   Remove from the oven and leave to cool for 5 minutes
before serving.

Steamed chocolate pudding

PREPARATION TIME 20 minutes   COOKING TIME 1¾ hours

SERVES 4–6

100g/3½oz butter, softened, plus extra for greasing
100g/3½oz/⅓ cup plus 4 tsp caster sugar
2 eggs, lightly beaten
100g/3½oz/¾ cup plus 1 tbsp self-raising flour
2 tbsp cocoa powder
100g/3½oz dark chocolate, melted
2 tbsp milk
1 recipe quantity Rich Chocolate Sauce (see page 188) or Espresso Chocolate Sauce (see page 191)

1   Grease a 1.25-litre/44fl oz/5-cup capacity pudding basin with butter. In a large bowl, beat the butter and sugar together until light and creamy, using an electric hand mixer, then add the eggs a little at a time until smooth. Sift the flour and cocoa together, and fold into the mixture with the chocolate and milk.

2   Spoon into the prepared basin and cover with a double layer of foil secured with string. Place the basin in a large saucepan and fill with water to come halfway up the side of the basin. Bring the water to the boil, turn down to a simmer and steam the pudding for 1¾ hours, adding extra boiling water as required.

3   Remove the basin from the saucepan and leave to cool for 10 minutes then turn the pudding out on to a serving plate. Serve with one of the chocolate sauces.

Pain-au-chocolat pudding

PREPARATION TIME 15 minutes   COOKING TIME 40–45 minutes

6 mini or 3 large pains au
   chocolat
5 eggs
1 tsp vanilla essence
100g/3½oz/⅓ cup plus 4 tsp
   caster sugar
1.5 litres/52fl oz/6 cups milk
pouring cream, for serving
   (optional)

1   Preheat the oven to 150°C/300°F/gas 2. Cut the
pains au chocolat into slices approximately 5mm/¼in
thick, and place them in the base of a 2-litre/70fl oz/
8 cup capacity ovenproof dish approximately 23cm/9in
in diameter.
2   In a large bowl, beat the eggs together with the vanilla
essence and sugar, using a hand whisk, and then whisk in
the milk.
3   Place the dish in a bain marie (see page 10) and bake
in the warm oven for 40–45 minutes, or until the sides
are firm but the middle is still slightly wobbly.
4   Remove the dish from the oven and leave to cool for
5 minutes before serving. Serve with cream, if wanted.

Chocolate & raspberry tart

PREPARATION TIME 20 minutes   COOKING TIME 35–40 minutes

MAKES 1 x 23cm/9in tart

1 x 23cm/9in Sweet Shortcrust
  Pastry case, baked (see
  page 15)
150g/5½oz dark chocolate,
  broken into pieces
75ml/2½fl oz/⅓ cup double
  cream
75g/2¾oz butter, chopped
2 eggs
3 tbsp plus 1 tsp caster sugar
1 tbsp golden syrup
125g/4½oz/1 cup raspberries,
  plus extra for serving
  (optional)
icing sugar, for dusting
1 recipe quantity Chocolate
  Marsala Cream (see
  page 193)

1   Preheat the oven to 150°C/300°F/gas 2. Place the baked pastry case on a baking tray.

2   In a small saucepan, melt the chocolate, cream and butter together over a low heat, then remove the pan from the heat and set aside to cool. In a large bowl, beat the eggs, sugar and golden syrup together for a few minutes until pale and light, using an electric hand mixer. Stir in the chocolate mixture, using a wooden spoon. Scatter the raspberries over the base of the tart, and pour the chocolate filling on top, taking care not to overfill.

3   Bake in the warm oven for 35-40 minutes, or until the middle of the tart is just set. Remove from the oven, and leave on the baking tray to cool completely.

4   Dust the tart with icing sugar just before serving, and serve with extra raspberries, if wanted, and some chocolate Marsala cream.

Tangy lemon & chocolate tarts

PREPARATION TIME 35 minutes   COOKING TIME 17–20 minutes

MAKES 4 x 10cm/4in tarts

4 x 10cm/4in Sweet Shortcrust
    Pastry cases, baked (see
    page 15)
juice and finely grated zest of
    3 lemons
150g/5½oz/⅔ cup caster
    sugar
5 eggs, lightly beaten
150g/5½oz butter, chopped
100g/3½oz dark chocolate,
    melted, plus shards to
    decorate
cocoa powder, sifted, for
    dusting

1 Preheat the oven to 180°C/350°F/gas 4. Place the
baked pastry cases on a baking tray.

2 Place the lemon juice and zest, the sugar, eggs and
butter in the top of a double boiler and heat, stirring
constantly with a wooden spoon, for approximately
15 minutes until the mixture thickens and coats the
back of the spoon. Remove from the heat and stir in the
melted chocolate. Pour the mixture into the baked pastry
cases, filling them about two-thirds full.

3 Bake in the hot oven for 12–15 minutes, or until
the custard is just firm. Remove from the oven and
leave the tarts on the tray to cool completely. Place a
shard of chocolate on each tart and dust with cocoa
just before serving.

White chocolate & berry tarts

PREPARATION TIME 30 minutes   COOKING TIME 8–10 minutes

MAKES 12 tarts

125g/4½oz butter, melted,
    plus extra for greasing
8 sheets filo pastry
5 tbsp caster sugar
150ml/5fl oz/⅔ cup double
    cream, whipped to soft
    peaks
125g/4½oz white chocolate,
    melted and left to cool
185g/6½oz/1½ cups
    mixed raspberries and
    blackberries

1   Preheat the oven to 180°C/350°F/gas 4. Grease a
12-hole muffin tin with butter.

2   Lay a sheet of filo pastry on the work surface and
brush with melted butter. Sprinkle over some of the sugar.
Place a second layer of pastry on top of the first layer,
lightly butter, then sprinkle with sugar. Repeat until all
of the layers have been used, finishing with a butter and
sugar layer. Cut the pastry stack into 12 squares and ease
a square into each hole of the muffin tin.

3   Bake in the hot oven for 8–10 minutes, or until the
pastry is golden brown. Remove from the oven and leave
the filo cases in the tin to cool.

4   For the filling, gently fold the cream and melted
chocolate together in a bowl, using a metal spoon. Remove
the tart cases from the tin and, just before serving, divide
the filling mixture evenly between them and spoon over the
mixed berries.

150

DEBERNY

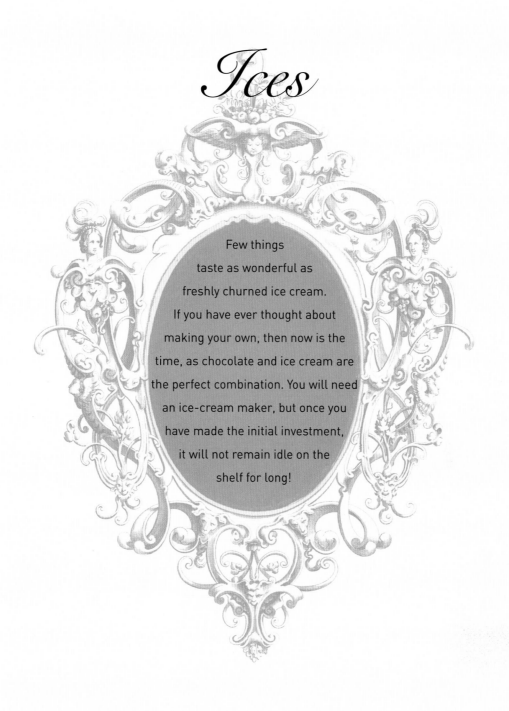

Ices

Few things
taste as wonderful as
freshly churned ice cream.
If you have ever thought about
making your own, then now is the
time, as chocolate and ice cream are
the perfect combination. You will need
an ice-cream maker, but once you
have made the initial investment,
it will not remain idle on the
shelf for long!

Rich chocolate ice cream

PREPARATION TIME 20 minutes, plus chilling and churning   COOKING TIME 5 minutes

MAKES 1 litre/35fl oz/4 cups

300ml/10½fl oz/1¼ cups milk
300ml/10½fl oz/1¼ cups
  double cream
350g/12oz dark or milk
  chocolate, broken into
  pieces
4 egg yolks
100g/3½fl oz/⅓ cup plus 4 tsp
  caster sugar

1 In a small saucepan, heat the milk, cream and chocolate together over a low heat until the chocolate has just melted. Remove the pan from the heat and stir with a wooden spoon until smooth.

2 In a large bowl, beat the egg yolks and sugar together, using a hand whisk, then pour in the hot chocolate mixture, whisking constantly. Return the mixture to the saucepan and heat, stirring constantly with a wooden spoon, until the mixture just begins to thicken and lightly coats the back of the spoon. Do not allow the mixture to boil, as it will curdle.

3 Remove from the heat, pour into a clean bowl and leave to cool completely. Refrigerate for 3 hours or overnight, then churn in an ice-cream machine according to the manufacturer's instructions.

Strawberry & white chocolate cheesecake ice cream

PREPARATION TIME 15 minutes, plus chilling and churning   MAKES 1 litre/35fl oz/4 cups

200g/7oz cream cheese,
　softened
150g/5½oz/⅔ cup caster sugar
250ml/9fl oz/1 cup double
　cream
250ml/9fl oz/1 cup sour cream
150g/5½oz/1 cup
　strawberries, chopped
125g/4½oz white chocolate,
　melted and left to cool

1   In a large bowl, beat the cream cheese and sugar together until soft, using an electric hand mixer. Whisk in the cream and sour cream, then stir in the strawberries and melted chocolate until just combined.

2   Refrigerate for 3 hours or overnight, then churn in an ice-cream machine according to the manufacturer's instructions.

Mint chocolate-chip ice cream

PREPARATION TIME 20 minutes, plus chilling and churning   COOKING TIME 5 minutes

MAKES 1 litre/35fl oz/4 cups

375ml/13fl oz/1½ cups milk
125g/4½oz/½ cup plus 2 tsp
  caster sugar
375ml/13fl oz/1½ cups double
  cream
175g/6oz dark chocolate,
  grated
2 tsp peppermint essence
2–3 drops green colouring
  (optional)

1   In a medium-sized saucepan, heat the milk and sugar together over a medium heat until the sugar has dissolved. Pour into a clean bowl and add the cream. Leave the mixture to cool completely before stirring in the chocolate, peppermint essence and green colouring, if using.

2   Refrigerate for 3 hours or overnight, then churn in an ice-cream machine according to the manufacturer's instructions.

Ginger & chocolate ice cream

PREPARATION TIME 25 minutes, plus chilling and churning   COOKING TIME 5 minutes

MAKES 1 litre/35fl oz/4 cups

250ml/9fl oz/1 cup milk
100g/3½oz dark chocolate,
  broken into pieces
3 egg yolks
100g/3½oz/⅓ cup plus 4 tsp
  caster sugar
500ml/17fl oz/2 cups double
  cream
100g/3½oz stem ginger,
  chopped
1 tbsp syrup from stem
  ginger jar

1   In a small saucepan, heat the milk and chocolate together over a low heat until just melted.

2   In a large bowl, beat the egg yolks and sugar together, using a hand whisk, then pour in the hot chocolate mixture, whisking constantly. Return the mixture to the saucepan and heat, stirring constantly with a wooden spoon, until the mixture just begins to thicken and lightly coats the back of the spoon. Do not allow the mixture to boil, as it will curdle.

3   Remove from the heat, pour into a clean bowl and leave to cool completely, then stir in the cream, ginger and ginger syrup. Refrigerate for 3 hours or overnight, then churn in an ice-cream machine according to the manufacturer's instructions.

Chocolate sorbet

PREPARATION TIME 30 minutes, plus chilling and churning   COOKING TIME 25 minutes

MAKES 1 litre/35fl oz/4 cups

250g/9oz/1 cup plus 4 tsp
  caster sugar
150g/5½oz cocoa powder,
  sifted
2 tsp vanilla essence

1 In a large saucepan, mix together the sugar and
900ml/33fl oz/3¾ cups water over a medium heat,
stirring well until the sugar has dissolved. Whisk in the
cocoa, using a hand whisk. Bring to the boil, then reduce
the heat and simmer for 20 minutes over a low heat,
stirring occasionally. Remove from the heat, pour into
a clean bowl and add the vanilla essence, then leave
to cool completely.

2 Refrigerate for 2 hours or overnight, then churn in
an ice-cream machine according to the manufacturer's
instructions.

White chocolate & raspberry parfait

PREPARATION TIME 25 minutes, plus freezing   COOKING TIME 5 minutes

125ml/4fl oz/½ cup double
  cream
125g/4½oz white chocolate,
  broken into pieces
2 egg whites
100g/3½oz/⅓ cup plus 4 tsp
  caster sugar
125g/4½oz/1 cup raspberries,
  lightly crushed, plus extra,
  whole, for serving
1 tbsp strawberry or
  raspberry liqueur

1   In a small saucepan, heat the cream and chocolate together over a low heat until just melted, then set aside to cool. In a large bowl, whisk the egg whites until soft peaks form, using an electric hand mixer, then gradually add the sugar until the mixture is thick and shiny. Fold in the chocolate cream, raspberries and liqueur, and divide evenly between 4 x 200ml/7fl oz/¾ cup moulds. Freeze the parfaits for 3 hours or overnight.

2   Remove the parfaits from the freezer, turn out on to individual plates and serve with the extra raspberries.

Grilled pineapple, macadamia & chocolate sundaes

PREPARATION TIME 15 minutes   COOKING TIME 5 minutes

1 small, ripe pineapple,
  peeled
100g/3½oz/⅓ cup plus 2 tsp
  soft brown sugar
2 tbsp dark rum
8 scoops Rich Chocolate Ice
  Cream (see page 146) or
  good-quality bought ice
  cream, slightly softened
1 recipe quantity Chocolate
  Rum Sauce (see page 191)
85g/3oz/½ cup macadamia
  nuts, roasted and chopped
4 ice-cream wafers (optional)

1   Cut the pineapple into quarters and remove the core, then slice into 1cm/½in slices. Place the slices in a large bowl with the brown sugar and dark rum and toss until well combined.

2   Place the pineapple slices on an oven tray under a hot grill for a few minutes until the pineapple has warmed slightly and has a light glaze.

3   Divide the grilled pineapple slices between 4 plates and top each one with 2 scoops of chocolate ice cream and the chocolate rum sauce. Sprinkle with chopped macadamia nuts and serve with ice-cream wafers, if using.

Peach & amaretti sundae with chocolate

PREPARATION TIME 30 minutes, plus cooling   COOKING TIME 15–17 minutes

150g/5½oz/⅔ cup caster sugar
4 ripe, firm, yellow peaches
8 scoops Rich Chocolate Ice
    Cream (see page 146) or
    good-quality bought ice
    cream, slightly softened
1 recipe quantity Rich
    Chocolate Sauce (see
    page 188)
100g/3½oz amaretti biscuits,
    crushed

1   In a small saucepan, heat the sugar and 250ml/9fl oz/1 cup water together over a medium heat until the sugar has dissolved, stirring frequently with a metal spoon. Bring to a simmer, then add the peaches and cook for 8–10 minutes until just tender. Remove the peaches from the syrup using a slotted spoon and set aside in a bowl to cool completely, then peel, cut in half horizontally and remove the stones.

2   Return the syrup to the heat and bring to the boil, then simmer until the syrup has reduced by half. Pour into a bowl and leave to cool.

3   Divide the peach halves equally between 4 dishes and spoon over some of the syrup. Place a scoop of chocolate ice cream on each peach half, top with some rich chocolate sauce and sprinkle over the crushed amaretti biscuits.

Frozen chocolate yogurt

PREPARATION TIME 20 minutes, plus chilling and churning   COOKING TIME 5 minutes

MAKES 1 litre/35fl oz/4 cups

100g/3½oz/⅓ cup plus 4 tsp
  caster sugar
1 tbsp cornflour
375ml/13fl oz/1½ cups milk
1 egg, lightly beaten
125ml/4fl oz/½ cup chocolate
  sauce
1 tbsp honey
375ml/13fl oz/1½ cups plain
  or vanilla-flavoured yogurt
1 tsp vanilla essence

1 In a small bowl, mix the sugar and cornflour to a paste using a little of the milk. Place the remaining milk in a small saucepan over a low heat and, using a hand whisk, whisk in the cornflour mixture and the egg. Continue to heat, stirring constantly with a wooden spoon, until the mixture thickens and coats the back of the spoon. Pour the mixture into a clean bowl and stir in the chocolate syrup and honey. Set aside until cold, then refrigerate for 3 hours.

2 Whisk in the yogurt and vanilla essence, using a hand whisk, then churn in an ice-cream machine according to the manufacturer's instructions.

Chocolate treats & drinks

Handmade chocolates and truffles are ideal for that extra-special occasion, and make beautiful gifts for friends and family. Chocolate drinks – from comforting Hot Chocolate to warm up a cold winter's night, to a divine Iced Mocha Shake for hot summer days – are the perfect indulgent treat.

Cranberry & port chocolate truffles

PREPARATION TIME 25 minutes, plus chilling   COOKING TIME 5 minutes

MAKES 30 truffles

200g/7oz dark chocolate, broken into pieces
60ml/2fl oz/¼ cup double cream
2 tbsp port
4 tbsp dried cranberries, chopped
250g/9oz white chocolate, melted and left to cool

1 In a small saucepan, combine the chocolate and cream over a low heat until the chocolate has just melted, stirring frequently with a wooden spoon. Remove from the heat and stir until smooth, then add the port and dried cranberries. Pour into a clean bowl and leave to cool completely, then refrigerate for approximately 30 minutes until firm.

2 Roll teaspoonfuls of the mixture in the melted white chocolate to form balls, put on a baking tray lined with baking paper and refrigerate for 1 hour until firm.

White chocolate, citrus & coconut truffles

PREPARATION TIME 25 minutes, plus chilling   COOKING TIME 5 minutes

MAKES 30 truffles

100ml/3½fl oz/⅓ cup coconut cream
350g/12oz white chocolate, broken into pieces
2 tsp lemon zest, finely grated
2 tsp lime zest, finely grated
2 tbsp coconut rum liqueur
90g/3¼oz/1 cup desiccated coconut

1   In a small saucepan, combine the coconut cream and chocolate together over a low heat until just melted, stirring frequently with a wooden spoon. Remove from the heat, and stir until smooth. Pour into a clean bowl and leave to cool, then stir in the lemon and lime zests and liqueur. Refrigerate for approximately 30 minutes until firm.

2   Roll teaspoonfuls of the mixture in the desiccated coconut to form balls. Place on a baking tray lined with baking paper and refrigerate for 1 hour until firm.

Peanut butter & milk chocolate truffles

PREPARATION TIME 30 minutes, plus chilling   COOKING TIME 5 minutes   MAKES 30 truffles

200g/7oz milk chocolate, broken into pieces
100ml/3½fl oz/⅓ cup double cream
3 tbsp crunchy peanut butter
100g/3½oz/⅔ cup roasted peanuts, crushed

1   In a small saucepan, combine the chocolate and cream over a low heat until the chocolate has just melted, stirring frequently with a wooden spoon. Remove from the heat, add the peanut butter and stir until smooth. Pour into a clean bowl and leave to cool completely, then refrigerate for approximately 30 minutes until firm.
2   Roll rounded teaspoonfuls of the mixture in the crushed peanuts, then place on a baking tray lined with baking paper and refrigerate for 1 hour until firm.

Double chocolate truffles

PREPARATION TIME 25 minutes, plus chilling   COOKING TIME 5 minutes   MAKES 20 truffles

150g/5½oz dark chocolate, broken into pieces
4 tbsp double cream
2 tbsp liqueur of your choice (e.g. Kahlua, Grand Marnier)
2 tbsp cocoa powder, sifted

1   In a small saucepan, combine the chocolate and cream over a low heat until the chocolate has just melted, stirring frequently with a wooden spoon. Remove from the heat and add your chosen liqueur. Pour the mixture into a clean bowl and leave to cool completely, then refrigerate for approximately 30 minutes until firm.
2   Roll teaspoonfuls of the mixture into small balls and toss in the cocoa to coat. Place the balls on a tray lined with baking paper and refrigerate for 1 hour until firm.

Chocolate & orange truffles

PREPARATION TIME 20 minutes, plus chilling   COOKING TIME 5 minutes   MAKES 18 truffles

150g/5½oz dark chocolate,
  broken into pieces
4 tbsp double cream
3 tbsp orange liqueur
zest of 1 orange, finely grated
icing sugar, sifted, for coating

1 In a small saucepan, combine the chocolate and cream over a low heat until the chocolate has just melted, stirring frequently with a wooden spoon. Remove from the heat and stir in the liqueur and orange zest, using a wooden spoon. Pour into a clean bowl and leave to cool completely, then refrigerate for approximately 30 minutes until firm.

2 Roll teaspoonfuls of the mixture into balls and coat with icing sugar. Place on a baking tray lined with baking paper and refrigerate for 1 hour until firm.

Gingernut & chocolate truffles

PREPARATION TIME 25 minutes, plus chilling   COOKING TIME 5 minutes   MAKES 30 truffles

300g/10½oz gingernut
  biscuits, finely crushed
3 tbsp cocoa powder
2 pieces stem ginger, finely
  chopped
250ml/9fl oz/1 cup condensed
  milk
90g/3¼oz/1 cup desiccated
  coconut

1 In a large bowl, mix together the biscuits, cocoa, stem ginger and condensed milk until well combined.

2 Using slightly wet hands, roll heaped teaspoonfuls of the mixture into balls and roll in the coconut to coat. Place on a baking tray lined with baking paper and refrigerate for 1 hour until firm.

Roasted almond drops (right)

PREPARATION TIME 15 minutes, plus chilling   COOKING TIME 5 minutes

MAKES 18 drops

200g/7oz dark or milk
  chocolate, broken into
  pieces
250g/9oz/2 cups slivered
  almonds, toasted

1   In a small saucepan, melt the chocolate over a low heat, stirring until smooth. Remove from the heat and stir in the toasted almonds until well combined.

2   Leave to cool for 5 minutes, then place teaspoonfuls of the mixture on a baking tray lined with baking paper and refrigerate for approximately 30 minutes until firm.

Roasted macadamia & ginger white chocolate drops

PREPARATION TIME 15 minutes, plus chilling   COOKING TIME 5 minutes   MAKES 18 drops

200g/7oz white chocolate,
  broken into pieces
160g/5½oz/1 cup whole
  macadamia nuts, roasted
3 pieces stem ginger, finely
  chopped

1   In a small saucepan, melt the chocolate over a low heat, stirring until smooth. Add the nuts and ginger, and stir to combine, using a wooden spoon.

2   Place teaspoonfuls of the mixture on a baking tray lined with baking paper to create neat drops, then refrigerate for approximately 30 minutes until firm.

Mint chocolate fudge

PREPARATION TIME 30 minutes, plus chilling   COOKING TIME 5 minutes

MAKES 16 squares

350g/12oz dark chocolate,
  broken into pieces
397g/14oz tin condensed milk
175g/6oz/1⅓ cups plus 4 tbsp
  icing sugar
2 tsp vanilla essence
1 tbsp peppermint essence

1   Line a shallow 23cm/9in square cake tin with
baking paper.

2   In a small saucepan, combine the chocolate and
condensed milk over a low heat until just melted. Remove
from the heat and stir until smooth, using a wooden
spoon, then stir in the sugar and both essences.

3   Pour the fudge mixture into the prepared tin and leave
to cool completely, then refrigerate for approximately 30
minutes until firm. Turn out of the tin using the paper
to help you, before cutting the fudge into squares, using
a sharp knife.

Cappuccino slims

PREPARATION TIME 15 minutes, plus chilling   COOKING TIME 5 minutes

MAKES 16 squares

200/7oz dark chocolate,
    broken into pieces
1 tsp instant coffee granules
1 tbsp coffee liqueur
150g/5½oz white chocolate,
    broken into pieces
2 tsp cocoa powder, sifted

1 Line a shallow 23cm/9in square cake tin with baking paper, letting the edges overhang the sides of the tin.

2 In a small saucepan, heat the dark chocolate over a low heat until just melted, then remove from the heat and stir until smooth, using a wooden spoon. Stir in the coffee and liqueur. Spread the mixture over the base of the prepared tin using a palette knife, and refrigerate for approximately 30 minutes until firm.

3 In a small saucepan, heat the white chocolate over a low heat until melted, then spread it over the dark chocolate mixture using a palette knife. Dust the top with cocoa.

4 Refrigerate for 30 minutes, then remove from the refrigerator and turn out from the tin, using the paper to help you, before cutting into squares with a knife that has been dipped in hot water first to warm it.

Chocolate-dipped dried fruits

PREPARATION TIME 15 minutes, plus chilling   COOKING TIME 5 minutes

MAKES 24 chocolates

250g/9oz dark chocolate,
   broken into pieces
24 pieces dried fruit,
   including apricots, pear
   and pineapple

1 In a small saucepan, heat the chocolate over a low heat until just melted, then remove from the heat and stir until smooth.

2 Wipe the dried fruit with paper towels, and dip each piece in the melted chocolate to cover halfway. (If the chocolate runs off without making a nice coating, leave it to cool for a few minutes, then try again.)

3 Place the dipped fruit on a baking tray lined with baking paper, and refrigerate for approximately 30 minutes until the chocolate has set.

Chocolate florentines

PREPARATION TIME 35 minutes   COOKING TIME 6–8 minutes

MAKES 24 florentines

50g/1¾oz butter, plus extra
    for greasing
3 tbsp plus 1 tsp caster sugar
2 tsp clear honey
50g/1¾oz/½ cup flaked
    almonds
50g/1¾oz/¼ cup red glacé
    cherries, chopped
50g/1¾oz/⅓ cup sultanas
150g/5½oz milk chocolate,
    melted and cooled

1   Preheat the oven to 180°C/350°F/gas 4. Line 2 large baking trays with baking paper.

2   In a small saucepan, melt the butter, sugar and honey together over a low heat until melted. Remove the pan from the heat. In a large bowl, mix together the almonds, glacé cherries and sultanas, then pour the butter mixture into the bowl, stirring well with a wooden spoon to combine. Place tablespoonfuls of the mixture on the baking tray, leaving 5cm/2in between them for room to spread, and press down lightly to flatten the mixture into rounds.

3   Bake in the hot oven for 6–8 minutes, or until lightly golden. Remove the trays from the oven, allow the florentines to cool for 5 minutes, then transfer them to a wire rack to cool completely.

4   When cold, turn the biscuits over (the backs will be smooth), and spread with melted chocolate. Once the chocolate has cooled slightly, make lines using a fork or wavy icing spreader. Leave on the baking tray until the chocolate is set.

Chocolate gingernut squares

PREPARATION TIME 25 minutes, plus chilling   COOKING TIME 5 minutes

MAKES 16 squares

400g/14oz dark chocolate,
  broken into pieces
125g/4½oz butter, chopped
397g/14oz can condensed
  milk
5 pieces stem ginger, finely
  chopped
250g/9oz gingernut biscuits,
  crushed
75g/2¾oz/¾ cup desiccated
  coconut, toasted, plus
  3 tbsp for sprinkling

1   Line a shallow 23cm/9in square cake tin with kitchen foil, leaving enough at the edges to overhang the sides.

2   In a small saucepan, heat the chocolate and butter together until just melted, then remove from the heat and stir until smooth. Stir in the remaining ingredients, and spoon into the prepared tin. Sprinkle with the extra coconut.

3   Refrigerate the chocolate gingernut mixture until firm. Remove from the fridge and turn out of the tin, using the foil to help you, then cut into squares with a sharp knife.

Chocolate & almond truffle squares

PREPARATION TIME 25 minutes, plus chilling   COOKING TIME 5 minutes   MAKES 16 squares

450g/1lb dark chocolate,
    broken into pieces
125ml/4fl oz/½ cup double
    cream
3 tbsp amaretto liqueur
50g/1¾oz/⅓ cup roasted
    almonds, roughly chopped

1 Line a shallow 20cm/8in square cake tin with kitchen foil.

2 In a small saucepan, heat 350g/12oz of the chocolate with the cream over a low heat until just melted. Remove the pan from the heat and stir until smooth, using a wooden spoon. Stir in the amaretto, then leave the mixture to one side.

3 In a clean pan, melt the remaining chocolate separately over a low heat. Spread half of the melted chocolate over the base of the prepared tin.

4 Refrigerate the chocolate base until firm, then top with the truffle mixture and sprinkle with the almonds. Drizzle the remaining melted chocolate over the truffle mixture in a decorative pattern. Refrigerate for approximately 30 minutes until firm, then turn out using the foil to help you, before cutting into squares with a sharp knife.

Best-ever hot chocolate

PREPARATION TIME 15 minutes   COOKING TIME 5 minutes

250ml/9fl oz/1 cup milk
250ml/9fl oz/1 cup double
   cream
2 tbsp caster sugar
125g/4½oz dark chocolate,
   broken into pieces
cocoa powder, sifted for
   dusting (optional)

1   Heat the milk and half the cream in a saucepan until just boiling. Remove from the heat and beat in the sugar and chocolate, using an electric hand mixer.

2   Divide the chocolate milk equally between 4 small cups (the mixture is very rich). Whip the remaining cream until it forms soft peaks, using an electric hand mixer, then place a tablespoonful on each cup and dust with cocoa powder, if using. Serve immediately.

Nutty chocolate coffee

PREPARATION TIME 5 minutes   COOKING TIME 5 minutes

1 litre/35fl oz/4 cups milk
4 tsp cocoa powder
4 tsp instant coffee granules
4 tbsp caster sugar
4 tbsp hazelnut liqueur
125ml/4floz/½ cup double
   cream, whipped to soft
   peaks
pinch cinnamon, to sprinkle

1 In a medium-sized saucepan, heat the milk until just boiling. Remove from the heat and whisk in the cocoa, coffee, sugar and liqueur.

2 Strain the mixture into a clean jug and divide equally between 4 cups. Top each cup with a tablespoonful of the whipped cream, then sprinkle over the cinnamon.

Chocolate Irish coffee

PREPARATION TIME 10 minutes

3 tbsp cocoa powder
875ml/30fl oz/3½ cups freshly
   brewed coffee
4 tsp caster sugar
2 tbsp Irish whisky
4 tbsp Chocolate Chantilly
   Cream (see page 194)
3 tbsp grated dark chocolate

1 Place the cocoa in a bowl and blend to a paste with 125ml/4fl oz/½ cup of the coffee. Whisk in the remaining coffee, the sugar and whisky, using a hand whisk.

2 Divide the coffee mixture evenly between 4 heatproof glasses. Top each glass with a tablespoonful of chocolate Chantilly cream, then sprinkle with the grated dark chocolate.

Iced mocha shake

PREPARATION TIME 20 minutes, plus chilling

875ml/30fl oz/3½ cups hot, strong coffee
3 tbsp cocoa powder
2 tbsp caster sugar
4 scoops Rich Chocolate Ice Cream (see page 146) or good-quality bought ice cream
125ml/4floz/½ cup double cream, whipped to soft peaks
4 tbsp grated dark chocolate

1 Pour the coffee into a large bowl. In a small bowl, mix the cocoa to a paste with 2 tablespoonfuls of the coffee. Whisk the paste back into the remaining coffee, with the sugar, using a hand whisk, then stir well with a wooden spoon until the sugar is dissolved. Leave to cool completely, then refrigerate for 30 minutes.

2 Place a scoop of ice cream in the bottom of each of 4 tall glasses. Pour over the coffee, dividing it equally between the glasses. Spoon a generous tablespoonful of the whipped cream over the top of each glass, then sprinkle with grated chocolate. Serve immediately.

Divine iced mint chocolate (right)

PREPARATION TIME 5 minutes

75g/2¾oz dark or milk
  chocolate, melted and left
  to cool
400ml/14fl oz/1⅔ cups cold
  milk
150ml/5fl oz/⅔ cup natural or
  vanilla-flavoured yogurt
6 mint leaves, plus extra to
  decorate
4 scoops Rich Chocolate Ice
  Cream (see page 146)
  or good-quality bought
  ice cream

1   Place the chocolate, milk, yogurt and mint in a
blender; combine until smooth.
2   Divide the milk mixture equally between 4 tall glasses
and top with a scoop of chocolate ice cream. Decorate
with mint leaves and serve immediately.

Chocolate milkshakes

PREPARATION TIME 5 minutes

500m/17fl oz/2 cups cold milk
1 tsp vanilla essence
4 tbsp chocolate sauce
8 tbsp Rich Chocolate Ice
  Cream (see page 146)
  or good-quality bought
  ice cream

1   Combine all of the ingredients in a blender and
process until well combined.
2   Divide the milkshake mixture equally between 4 glasses.

150

Sauces, icings & frostings

These recipes deserve a chapter devoted just to them as you will use them time and time again. While a number of the recipes throughout the book suggest a sauce, frosting or icing, feel free to mix and match. All of the recipes are simple to make and will transform a favourite dessert into something special.

Rich chocolate sauce (right)

PREPARATION TIME 10 minutes   COOKING TIME 5 minutes

MAKES 375ml/13fl oz/1½ cups

250ml/9fl oz/1 cup double
  cream
150g/5½oz dark chocolate,
  broken into pieces
1 tbsp chocolate liqueur
  (optional)
1 tbsp icing sugar
1 tsp vanilla essence

1 In a small saucepan, combine the cream and chocolate over a low heat, stirring with a wooden spoon until smooth. Remove the pan from the heat.

2 Stir in the liqueur, if using, sugar and vanilla essence. Serve warm.

White chocolate sauce

PREPARATION TIME 10 minutes   COOKING TIME 5 minutes

MAKES 375ml/13fl oz/1½ cups

250ml/9fl oz/1 cup double
  cream
125g/4½oz white chocolate,
  broken into pieces
1 tsp vanilla essence

1 In a small saucepan, combine the cream and chocolate over a low heat until the chocolate has just melted. Add the vanilla essence and stir until smooth, using a wooden spoon.

2 Remove the pan from the heat and serve warm.

Chocolate rum sauce

PREPARATION TIME 10 minutes   COOKING TIME 5 minutes

MAKES 300ml/10½fl oz/1¼ cups

250ml/9fl oz/1 cup double
  cream
2 tsp granulated sugar
100g/3½oz dark chocolate,
  broken into pieces
2 tbsp dark rum

1   In a small saucepan, heat the cream, sugar and chocolate together over a low heat until the chocolate has melted, stirring with a wooden spoon until smooth.

2   Remove the pan from the heat, stir in the rum and serve warm.

Espresso chocolate sauce (left)

PREPARATION TIME 10 minutes   COOKING TIME 5 minutes

MAKES 375ml/13fl oz/1½ cups

250ml/9fl oz/1 cup double
  cream
150g/5½oz dark chocolate,
  broken into pieces
60ml/2fl oz/¼ cup hot,
  strong espresso coffee
1 tbsp coffee liqueur

1   In a small saucepan, combine the cream and chocolate over a low heat until the chocolate has just melted. Remove the pan from the heat.

2   Add the coffee and liqueur and set aside to cool for 10 minutes before serving.

Chocolate Marsala cream (left)

PREPARATION TIME 10 minutes   MAKES 250ml/9fl oz/1 cup

250ml/9fl oz/1 cup double
　cream
1 tbsp icing sugar
1 tbsp Marsala wine
cocoa powder, sifted, to dust

1　In a large bowl, combine the cream, icing sugar and
Marsala wine and whip to soft peaks, using an electric
hand mixer.

2　Dust with cocoa and serve immediately.

Chocolate mascarpone cream

PREPARATION TIME 10 minutes, plus chilling   MAKES 250ml/9fl oz/1 cup

125g/4½oz milk chocolate,
　melted and left to cool
1 tsp vanilla essence
125g/4oz mascarpone cheese

1　In a large bowl, whisk all the ingredients together,
using an electric hand mixer.

2　Refrigerate for 30 minutes before using.

Chocolate Chantilly cream

PREPARATION TIME 15 minutes   MAKES 250ml/9fl oz/1 cup

250ml/9fl oz/1 cup double
  cream
2 tbsp icing sugar
100g/3½oz dark or milk
  chocolate, melted and left
  to cool

1   In a large bowl, whip the cream and icing sugar together to form soft peaks, using an electric hand mixer.
2   Gently fold in the melted chocolate until just combined, before using.

Chocolate buttercream

PREPARATION TIME 15 minutes, plus chilling   MAKES 375ml/13fl oz/1½ cups

175g/6oz butter
200g/7oz/1 cup plus 1 tbsp
  soft brown sugar
1 egg yolk
1 tbsp milk
1 tbsp cocoa powder
100g/3½oz dark chocolate,
  melted and left to cool

1   In a large bowl, beat the butter and sugar together until light and fluffy, using an electric hand mixer. Add the remaining ingredients and continue beating until thick and light.
2   Refrigerate for 30 minutes before using.

Mocha buttercream

PREPARATION TIME 45 minutes, plus cooling and chilling   COOKING TIME 5 minutes

MAKES 500ml/17fl oz/2 cups

175ml/6fl oz/scant ¾ cup milk
100g/3½oz dark chocolate,
    broken into pieces
4 tsp instant coffee granules
1 tsp vanilla essence
3 egg yolks
100g/3½oz butter, softened
200g/7oz/1½ cups plus 4 tsp
    icing sugar

1   In a large saucepan, combine the milk, chocolate, coffee and vanilla essence over a low heat until the chocolate has just melted, then remove the pan from the heat. Beat the yolks in a bowl and whisk in the chocolate mixture. Return the mixture to the pan and cook, stirring constantly with a wooden spoon, until the mixture begins to thicken and coats the back of the spoon. Do not allow to boil. Pour the mixture into a bowl and set aside to cool for 30 minutes.

2   In a clean bowl, whisk the butter until light and creamy, using an electric hand mixer, then add the chocolate mixture with the icing sugar. Continue to whisk until thick and glossy. Refrigerate for 30 minutes before using.

Dark chocolate ganache (right)

PREPARATION TIME 5 minutes, plus cooling   COOKING TIME 5 minutes

MAKES 250ml/9fl oz/1 cup

175g/6oz dark chocolate,
   broken into pieces
25g/1oz butter
125ml/4fl oz/½ cup double
   cream

1   In a small saucepan, combine all of the ingredients over a low heat, and stir until the chocolate and butter have melted. Remove the pan from the heat.
2   Pour into a clean bowl and leave to cool for around 20 minutes, or until the mixture begins to thicken. Use as a filling or topping in your chosen cake recipe, or serve warm as a sauce.

White chocolate ganache

PREPARATION TIME 10 minutes, plus cooling   COOKING TIME 5 minutes

MAKES 250ml/9fl oz/1 cup

125ml/4fl oz/½ cup crème
   fraîche
125g/4½oz white chocolate,
   broken into pieces

1   In a small saucepan, heat the crème fraîche over a low heat. Remove the pan from the heat and add the white chocolate. Stir gently until the chocolate has melted, using a wooden spoon, then continue stirring for a few more minutes until smooth.
2   Set aside to cool for 30 minutes, or until the ganache has thickened slightly.

Chocolate cream cheese frosting (left)

PREPARATION TIME 10 minutes   MAKES 375ml/13fl oz/1½ cups

250g/9oz cream cheese,
  softened
100g/3½oz dark chocolate,
  melted and left to cool
15g/½oz butter, softened
1 tsp vanilla essence
250g/9oz/2 cups icing sugar,
  sifted

1 In a large bowl, beat the cream cheese until light,
using an electric hand mixer.
2 Add the melted chocolate, butter, vanilla essence
and icing sugar, and continue beating until creamy and
thickened.

Chocolate rum frosting

PREPARATION TIME 15 minutes   MAKES 375ml/13fl oz/1½ cups

100g/3½oz dark chocolate,
  broken into pieces
25g/1oz butter, chopped
300g/10½oz/2⅓ cups icing
  sugar
100ml/3½fl oz/⅓ cup double
  cream
2 tbsp dark or light rum
1 tsp vanilla essence

1 In a small saucepan, combine the chocolate and butter
together over a low heat, and stir until smooth.
2 Place the icing sugar in a large bowl and, using a
wooden spoon, mix in the chocolate mixture, cream, rum
and vanilla essence. Whisk until thick, using an electric
hand mixer.

Chocolate fudge frosting

PREPARATION TIME 15 minutes   COOKING TIME 5 minutes

MAKES 375ml/13fl oz/1½ cups

75g/2¾oz dark chocolate,
  broken into pieces
75g/2¾oz butter, chopped
250g/9oz/2 cups icing sugar
2 tbsp cocoa powder
5 tbsp milk
1 tsp vanilla essence

1   In a small saucepan, heat the chocolate and butter over a low heat until just melted. In a medium-sized bowl, mix the icing sugar and cocoa together, and pour the melted chocolate over. Add the milk and vanilla essence, and stir to combine well.

2   Put the bowl containing the mixture into a larger bowl containing a little iced water and beat the mixture with a wooden spoon until it is thick enough to spread and hold its shape.

White chocolate frosting

PREPARATION TIME 10 minutes, plus cooling and chilling   COOKING TIME 5 minutes
MAKES 375ml/13fl oz/1½ cups

100g/3½oz white chocolate,
   broken into pieces
250ml/9fl oz/1 cup double
   cream
250g/9oz mascarpone cheese

1   In a small saucepan, combine the chocolate and
150ml/5fl oz/⅔ cup of the cream over a low heat until
the chocolate has just melted. Remove the pan from
the heat, and stir until smooth. Pour the mixture into
a clean bowl and leave to cool for 30 minutes, stirring
occasionally, then refrigerate for approximately 1 hour.
2   In a large bowl, stir the mascarpone until smooth,
using a wooden spoon. Add the chocolate mixture and
as much of the remaining cream as required to make a
spreading consistency.

Shiny chocolate icing (right)

PREPARATION TIME 15 minutes   MAKES 250ml/9fl oz/1 cup

400g/14oz/3 cups icing sugar
2 tbsp cocoa powder
15g/½oz butter, softened

1 Place the icing sugar and cocoa in a bowl and make a small well in the middle. Place the butter in the well and pour over 2½ tbsp boiling water. Stir until the butter has melted, then continue stirring until the icing is of spreading consistency, adding about another 2½ tbsp water as required. Use immediately.

Creamy chocolate icing

PREPARATION TIME 10 minutes   MAKES 250ml/9fl oz/1 cup

225g/8oz/1¾ cups icing sugar
3 tbsp cocoa powder
25g/1oz butter, melted
4–5 tbsp milk

1 Sift the icing sugar and cocoa into a bowl.
2 Stir in the butter and enough of the milk to make a creamy consistency.

Index